HULDAH BUNTAIN:

Woman of Courage

Hal Donaldson & Kenneth M. Dobson

Huldah Buntain: Woman of Courage
Hal Donaldson and Kenneth M. Dobson

Printed in the United States of America
ISBN: 1-880689-04-9
Copyright 1995, Onward Books, Inc.

Cover design by Matt Key

Unless otherwise noted, Scripture quotations are taken from *The Living Bible*, copyright 1971 by Tyndale House Publishers, Wheaton, Illinois. Scripture quotations marked NIV are taken from the *New International Version*. Copyright 1973, 1978, 1984, International Bible Society. Scripture quotations marked KJV are taken from the *King James Version* of the Bible.

Excerpt from *Treasures in Heaven* reprinted by permission of Whitaker House, Springdale, PA. Copyright 1989 by Calcutta Mission of Mercy.

Acknowledgments

Special thanks to Deb Petrosky, Matt Key, Chuck Goldberg, Gary and Shirley Speer, Dan McDaniel, Don Beard, Dan Scherling, Shari Henson, Rochelle Gracias, Tyrone Thompson, Rajendra Pillai, V. Satya Narayan, Denzel Wood, and Solomon Wang.

Dedication

Dedicated to David Burdine and Bethesda Outreach Ministries.

Endorsements

I remember waiting at the Seattle-Tacoma airport for my connecting flight to Vancouver, British Columbia, where I would speak on behalf of the family at the Canadian memorial service for Dr. Mark Buntain. I wondered what words of comfort could be shared with my recently widowed Aunt Huldah, who would soon arrive to make the same airline connection.

Memories of Auntie Huldah—and her lifetime of service—flooded me. As a young boy, I remember my family reading her letters at the dinner table. How difficult it must be to live in India, I thought, even at my tender age. Their missionary furlough years, which had been filled with the joy of reacquainting our families, always ended the same way—with tears and no hope of seeing each other for another four or five years. Saying good-bye to her family in Canada always pained Auntie Huldah.

At age 19, I lived with Auntie Huldah and Uncle Mark for six months when my cousin Bonnie left to attend Evangel College. While seeing 10 million refugees migrate from Bangladesh to West Bengal, I felt my heart break for suffering humanity. At that time God called me into the ministry. That experience so permanently impacted my human and spiritual senses that I never forgot what life in Calcutta was like.

I wondered what life would be like for Huldah now —in India, so far from family, and alone. Surely, if anyone deserves to retire from ministry, it is Auntie Huldah.

When she arrived at the airport, her countenance was etched with the deep sense of loss and pain that one might expect from a woman who had just lost her husband. During our visit in Canada over the next few days, however, her resolve to finish the work she had been called to amazed me. I don't know why I was so astounded. Perhaps I always thought it was mostly Mark's spiritual fortitude that had kept their passion for India burning so strongly.

I've often said, "The real mark of spiritual maturity is not seen on the mountaintops, but in the valleys." On that brief visit to Canada, I realized the spiritual greatness within my aunt had been there all along. Her dedication surpassed that of a faithful wife who honored her wedding vows. At some point, many years ago, Huldah Buntain had stood face to face with her Maker. When she said, "Lord, I surrender all," it was not conditional.

Her decision brought incredible loss and restricted many of her choices. Despite the pain, the loneliness, and the overwhelming uncertainty of her future,

Huldah's unwavering choice to make Christ both Savior and Lord impacted her decisions during her walk in the valley.

In a day when discipleship is often compromised, Huldah Buntain stands tall as an example of what authentic commitment is all about.

I am proud to be her nephew.

Ken Dobson

We as a church want to do all we can to communicate the gospel but have found that raising up missionaries through training, motivation, and financing has not been the most effective. Since heaven and hell are real, and Jesus is the only solution to mankind's sin problem, we must maximize the effectiveness of every dollar. I encourage churches to simplify their approach and network with organizations like Mission of Mercy who facilitate churches like New Life Church to do just that.

By working with Mission of Mercy, we have the opportunity to network with a very effective organization that works in an area of the world we want to target. We could not get greater spiritual results from any other method of missions outreach.

Ted Haggard, Senior Pastor
New Life Church
Colorado Springs, CO

With both hands pressing on his lower abdomen, the late Mark Buntain said, "Wayne, you must come to visit Calcutta. I feel it way down here." Little did I realize the impact of his words and ministry on my life these many years later.

Seeing firsthand the eternal fruit of such faithful labor, it is truly our joy to join with others in supporting this tremendous work of God that gives hope to so many hurting people. Never have I witnessed a greater return of our church's missions investments.

E. Wayne Hanks, Senior Pastor
First Assembly of God
Garland, TX

If Jesus were in Calcutta, what do you think He would do? Of course He would preach the kingdom of heaven, heal the sick, and cast out devils.

Would that be all?

No. He would carry out the mission of mercy, as this is exactly what the Mission of Mercy does. Let us all support this noble work.

David Yonggi Cho, Pastor
Yoido Full Gospel Church
Seoul, South Korea

It is truly an honor to join hands with an organization of people whose hearts have remained so pure before the Lord and whose work has affected so much change. It is my daily goal to properly represent the vision shared by all those who diligently uphold the banner of this genuine *mission of mercy*.

Janet Paschal
Recording Artist
Nashville, TN

There are many agencies requesting assistance for the needy of our world. The question that often comes to me as a church leader is: "What agencies can be trusted?"

Mission of Mercy is one that can be trusted. We want every dollar to count for eternity, so Mission of Mercy is one of the outlets we use to fulfill our Lord's commission to "reach the world."

Confidence! Oh, what a good word in a day of distrust at almost every level.

Glen D. Cole, Superintendent
Northern California/Nevada District
Assemblies of God

Marilyn Hickey Ministries and Happy Church have been involved with Mission of Mercy for perhaps the past six years. It is a great joy to see what God is doing in Calcutta and way beyond what one can imagine.

I've visited over 60 countries, but I think the greatest missions outreach I have seen is in Calcutta. I appreciate the vision of this ministry and personally enjoy being a part of it.

Marilyn Hickey, President
Marilyn Hickey Ministries
Denver, CO

One of the greatest privileges in my life was co-laboring with the late Dr. Mark Buntain. Never have I met a man more genuine, full of zeal, with such a burning desire to reach the lost for Jesus Christ. Today Mission of Mercy still reflects his passion for souls and brings hope to a hurting world.

Jon F. Stemkoski, President
Stone Ministries, Inc.
Celebrant Singers

Contents

Foreword

Missionary legends are not made in a hurry, nor by accident. The term "a great missionary" only belongs to a lifetime of giving.

"A missionary with a great heart" describes the survivor of long, harrowing days and "a thousand midnights." It belongs to one who loves God and the godless and who knows no retreat. It is a title for the meek and the mighty, for the faithful and the daring, for the plodder and the doer, and for one who is neither daunted by the impossible nor detained by the plaudits of onlookers.

Missionary Huldah Buntain has, indeed, exemplified all of the above during more than 40 years of service to her Lord in Calcutta, India. The story told on the pages you have in your hands is the record of enduring love and unswerving devotion to the call of God. Huldah is a faithful servant of Jesus Christ and continues to serve her generation well.

She did it, for most of her life, at the side of a unique and sacrificing man of great devotion and gifts.

Her very effective place in partnership with Mark Buntain has always been noteworthy. Together they carried the burdens of enormous challenges and escalating victories.

When Mark was taken to His eternal place with the Lord whom he served, we all know that Huldah then stood before her greatest challenge. Our hearts "stood still" as she prayerfully reached, in faith, to accept the awesome calling of continuing alone.

Her story is a compelling and moving saga of missionary devotion, bravery, faith, and persistence. All of us in the long story of Assemblies of God missions take joy in recognizing a fellow servant of Jesus Christ who has shown God's love in one of the neediest places on the face of the earth. Authors Hal Donaldson and Kenneth M. Dobson have caught the essence of the heart and calling of a true missionary. We have all been enriched by the life and ministry of a "woman of courage," and now by the exquisite tenderness in the telling of the story.

Loren O. Triplett

Introduction

I vowed I would never return to Calcutta, India. After two previous visits, the city had haunted me with a myriad of uncomfortable emotions and unanswerable questions. I couldn't bear to trudge through a multitude of desperate brown-skinned children unless I could somehow rescue them.

How could I flee in a waiting taxi after peering into their dark, somber eyes? Couldn't I place new shoes on their archless, calloused feet? Couldn't I supply clean T-shirts to replace those showing the wear of countless monsoons? Couldn't I offer a bowl of rice to ease their hunger pangs and a glass of milk to cool their palates amidst the festering heat?

I didn't want to eat nutritious food and sleep in a warm bed, knowing thousands of hollow-eyed, gaunt-cheeked Indian children were dying within my reach. Some lived in clusters of mud huts known as bustees, which provided insufficient shelter from the slashing rains. Others roamed endlessly through the night, their feet infected by sores from traipsing the garbage-laden streets.

Traveling to Calcutta was more than an adventure; it was an introspective journey that would plant seeds of discomfort in my secure world.

But I did return because I love this crying city and the needy people of India. I returned because I yearned to see Jesus in action. Through Mark and Huldah Buntain and their Mission of Mercy, Jesus had dried the tears of Calcutta's people for 40 years. He had provided an education, clothing, and medical care for countless Indian children. He had fed thousands each day and offered hope to the lost and dying. Against the backdrop of sin and despair, Jesus had repelled the forces of darkness. Through the Buntains, He had shone His light of love and compassion. And Calcutta would never be the same.

Meeting Huldah

I hadn't seen Huldah since her husband Mark passed away five years earlier. It was apparent, however, that not much about the city or her leadership ability had changed. When I entered Huldah's office on Park Street in the heart of Calcutta's business district, it didn't surprise me to see her surrounded by staff members seeking her instructions and advice. She still worked at a pace fit for a Wall Street executive. Phones were ringing, papers shuffling, staff members racing.

Within moments, however, the administrator was transformed into a pastor and social worker. An aide burst into her office with urgency in his voice. On his heels, garbed in a tattered saree, was a mother clutching a puny baby.

"The baby isn't breathing right," the shaken aide stammered. "He isn't breathing right."

Huldah leapt to her feet and grabbed a telephone receiver. "Have a doctor waiting downstairs," she ordered. "We have a baby who is having difficulty breathing."

The frightened mother cradled her baby, her eyes pleading for help. I rubbed the child's copper-skinned forehead, attempting to awaken him from his listless state. He remained motionless. I put my ear next to the child's nose to make sure he was breathing. His breaths were irregular and strained.

Huldah scribbled instructions to the hospital staff on a pad of paper. She handed the note to the aide, then hurriedly escorted the mother and child to the elevator. Huldah prayed all the way down the hall. "Dear Jesus, touch this child. Please help him, Jesus," she repeated. "Please, dear Jesus. Save this child."

When we knew the mother and child were in the hands of medical professionals, we returned to her office.

"That was pretty amazing," I said with an astonished look. "Your office is like an emergency ward."

"That's a common occurrence around here," she replied. "These people have so many needs and no money to get treatment in other hospitals."

"Was that a voucher you handed to your aide—to authorize whatever care she needed?" I asked.

"Yes, there won't be any charge to that dear woman. She doesn't have any way of paying for the treatment. She'll get all the help she needs."

Woman of Compassion

I began the interview for this book only to be interrupted by a knock at the door. An associate pastor and his wife had come to seek Huldah's help in the face of a crisis: A family member was in the hospital with a life-threatening heart condition. Like a shepherdess Huldah offered comforting words; like a counselor she offered advice; like a mother she offered an embrace. The young couple left with renewed faith and peace.

"They still depend on you here, don't they, Huldah?" I asked, my tape recorder in hand.

Adjusting her glasses, she grinned like a proud parent. "I guess they do. Sometimes I'll walk through the hospital or step onto the street and the children will just cling to me. But when you put yourself in their position, you can't help but make yourself available and try to help them. Sometimes I invite them to my home and we'll have children all around the lunch table," she said cheerfully. "I love having them around. They're like my kids."

She proceeded to relate one story after another of children and teenagers who had come to her table to seek answers. I could almost see her patting their hands and offering soothing words. I could visualize her holding their hands and offering a prayer. Suddenly I could see in Huldah the same compassion I had observed in Mark on previous visits to their church and Mission. Her compassion wasn't something artificial, self-induced, or something a person could learn. It was supernatural—a gift from Almighty God.

A few days later I visited Mother Teresa's home for the destitute and dying. I was introduced to her as the author of two books on Mark and Huldah Buntain. Mother Teresa took my hand and smiled courteously, responding to Huldah's name as though this fellow servant were a saint. "Yes, she's my dear friend," Mother Teresa remarked. "She is carrying on a marvelous work."

That afternoon it was apparent to me that Huldah was doing far more than fulfilling her husband's dreams. She was a missionary in her own right, bent on fulfilling the vision God had placed on her heart: to expose millions to the love of Jesus in Calcutta and throughout India.

City of Despair

Calcutta is a desperate city. Four miles wide and nine miles long, Calcutta is home to 18 million people. Eighty percent of the city is slums. There are 1,000 people to every toilet and 5,000 to every drinking fountain.

Clapboard hovels, street vendors, beggars, half-naked children, and an estimated 40,000 human rickshaws fill the roads. Cows venerated as sacred monopolize the streets, forcing taxis and pedestrians from their path. Packs of pye dogs fight for scraps of food. Homeless men, women, and children lie on mats positioned in alleys and on patches of open pavement. Many are embroiled in a daily quest for survival, grown men jostling in line for a job that may pay 10 rupees a day (30 U.S. cents).

Disease is king in this city. Epidemics do not discriminate, snatching the lives of young and old. Cholera, typhoid, tetanus, and more keep hospitals and mortuaries busy.

Despite the poverty, threat of disease, and unsightly conditions, Mark and Huldah Buntain journeyed to the city in 1954 with their one-year-old daughter Bonnie. Huldah had compared approaching Calcutta by ship, up the narrow and treacherous Hooghly River, to entering the mouth of a dragon. In her book, *Treasures in Heaven,* she wrote:

> Gusts of warm air blew in my face like the exhaust of an automobile. With each breath I had to swallow the heavy, smoggy particles collecting in my throat. The murky water resembled sewage flowing down a wide gutter,

only this current contained dead dogs and cows and even the skeletal remains of a human body. Unclothed natives were bathing in the water. Other villagers congregated on the banks. It made me think of Tom Sawyer and Huckleberry Finn and the Mississippi Queen; then I realized the two settings had nothing in common.

Mark and [my] mother coughed in unison and covered their mouths with handkerchiefs. I held Bonnie against my breast, wondering if her fragile body could survive the lethal fumes. We were stunned to silence. I could see that even Mark appeared staggered by the dearth of poverty of these scantily-clad villagers. A slight paleness had seized his face....

I reluctantly walked off the ship, knowing each step was one foot closer to my internment in what I deemed a dark, primeval world....

As we shouldered through the crowd, children clamored at our ankles and begged for a coin or scrap of food. So many of them were skinny, puny, and deformed. I longed to gather them in my arms. Their eyes loomed like those of lofty owls, looking at me as if I were a majestic goddess here to deliver them from the cruelties of their world. Tears surfaced in my eyes, thinking to myself that some of the children who had touched me would soon be a bag of lifeless bones.... On the way to the mission house . . . the cries of the children we had left back at the dock were still ringing in my ears. I felt like a tyrannical empress who had elevated her nose in response to the pervading pleas....

The hovels surrounding the waterfront were like youngsters' forts found in the backyards of North American homes: cardboard, wood, plastic, and metal sheets pieced together. There were no calming meadows and timeless streams, no mossy brooks or passive ponds— only a blur of faces in bondage braced against walls matted with filth.

Women in threadbare rags, clutching malnourished babies, froze with venomous glares as our vehicle meandered through the chaotic streets. Two women in particular ignored our Caucasian faces. They were wearing shapely sarees, bracelets, anklets, and toe rings. Jewelry was dangling from their pierced ears and noses. These women seemed displaced, as if they were princesses banished from their palaces. Sharing the street with them were women and children whose wardrobes consisted of nothing more than sackcloth.

I disliked myself for having so much. I wanted
to empty my purse into the streets and toss my
garments and jewelry into the lap of a disheart-
ened mother so some of them, at least, would
have twenty-four hours to live like a queen....
I was incapable of carrying on a conversation. I
thought my world had surely come to an end.

With each passing day, Huldah's courage and
commitment to help the people of her new city
mounted. She fell in love with the Indian people, and
vowed to do everything in her power to rescue them
from their despair and introduce them to Jesus Christ.

Evangelistic services were held every night for five
years in a tent or rented hall until a church could be
built on a valuable strip of land on Royd Street.
There they ministered for four decades through a
wide range of outreaches. Enduring adversity and
devoid of Western comforts, they lived in obscurity
for many years. Their humble apartment was an
oasis from the misery outside their walls—a city
blanketed by gaseous vapors, smog, and suffocating
humidity. It was here that they raised their beautiful
daughter. There weren't an array of parks in which
to push a stroller, or community swimming pools to
find relief from the scorching sun. There weren't
restaurant chains to frequent or shopping malls to
while away a Saturday afternoon. This was Calcutta,
unlike any city on earth.

Leaving a Mark

The Buntains and their Mission—through a wide range of programs, churches, outreaches, schools, hospitals, feeding efforts, and more—have left the mark of Jesus Christ on the lives of countless thousands. But the miraculous stories are not confined to Calcutta's teeming millions. The influence of the Mission extends to regions throughout India, from bustling cities to remote villages. Because one man and woman obeyed the voice of God, thousands have been reached with the gospel and rescued from the clutches of hell.

It is apparent God's blessing continues to rest on this ministry—largely because Huldah refused to retreat to the West for a life of security and comfort after her husband's death. She found the courage to believe God would lead her as He had Mark. She believed He would multiply the work in Calcutta and give her the plan to reach far beyond the city limits into other areas of India. As you will discover in this book, God has honored the labor and faith of His chosen servant.

Mission of Mercy has become synonymous with compassion. The Creator so loved the nation of India that He sent a man, a woman, and many others through their prayers and gifts to be His hand extended to the hurting and diseased. This ministry represents the miraculous power of Almighty God, for no man or woman alone could conceive or achieve what is being accomplished in India. It was God who whispered to the Buntains, His hand that fed the hurting, His hand that guided the doctors. And, as the Buntains have always maintained, He alone deserves the glory.

Huldah Buntain: Woman of Courage is a remarkable story fit for a Hollywood screenplay. Yet it is more than an entertaining portrait. This is a testimony of what can be accomplished through servanthood and commitment. May those who read these pages be stirred to prayer and action. May they invite God to use them to rescue the perishing.

Hal Donaldson

CHAPTER ONE

Fallen Warrior

June 1989.

"Mark, you don't have to go with me to the airport," Huldah said, packing her suitcase for a flight to the States.

"I want to go," he said. "I want to see you off."

"It's too hot, and you need to stay off your feet," she reasoned. "Besides, you have a cold, and you'll have a long day tomorrow."

Mark pondered her suggestion. He knew their transport officer and others were available to escort her safely to the airport and through customs. Mark, a tall, round-faced man with distinguishable dark-rimmed glasses, had just returned from Germany and England, where he had held services on behalf of the Mission.

He wanted to accompany Huldah but desperately needed to shut his eyes. The arduous trip had sapped his strength.

Huldah could see the weariness showing around the edges of his eyes. "Mark, just go to sleep. I'll be fine."

"Are you sure you wouldn't mind?" he asked reluctantly.

"No, you rest. I'll call you tonight."

He embraced Huldah. "Okay, call me tonight."

Mark rolled onto the bed and watched as Huldah ran a brush through her blonde hair. "You're going to be late, Huldah. You'd better hurry."

Huldah half-turned, saying, "Okay, but make sure you're home at 9:00 tonight and I'll phone you." She knew he was prone to make his way to the hospital for pastoral visits or to a prayer room at all hours of the night.

Huldah exited. A moment later she returned.

"What did you forget?" Mark asked.

"I just want to make sure you're going to take care of yourself."

He responded, "I will, but you're going to be late."

"If you're not here when I call I'm going to be cross with you," she said, smiling and staring into his weary eyes. "Are you going to be okay?"

"I'm fine. I love you."

Huldah descended the steps to a waiting car filled with helpful staff members. They proceeded to the airport.

Collapsed

A short time later, a phone call awakened Mark from a deep sleep. He rose to pick up the receiver and passed out, his head colliding with the corner of the bed.

The houseboy, hearing the phone buzzing off the hook, knocked on the bedroom door. "Sahib, Sahib?"

There was no response.

He knocked again. Finally he poked his head inside only to find Mark, still conscious, collapsed on the tile floor.

"What happened?" the houseboy stammered.

"I fell," Mark said awkwardly.

The houseboy and a helper lifted Mark to his bed and helped him get dressed. Then Mark phoned the hospital.

"This is Pastor; I'm not well," he said to a hospital telephone operator in a vague tone.

"Shall I send a car or an ambulance?" she asked nervously.

Mark sighed deeply as if trying to form the words for a reply. "You better send an ambulance; please hurry."

"Jesus . . . Jesus . . . Jesus," a white-faced Mark repeated until the ambulance arrived.

Medical personnel placed Mark on a stretcher. One of his eyes began to flutter, his eyesight blurring. By the time he was downstairs, his speech was slurred. By the time he arrived at the hospital, he was experiencing convulsions.

Five hours later he was rushed into surgery.

Huldah in Bangkok

Upon entering her hotel room in Bangkok, Thailand, en route to the States, Huldah noticed the red light flashing on the telephone. She retrieved a message from the hotel operator to call Dr. Jim Long—their daughter Bonnie's husband and a prominent heart specialist in the United States.

Jim relayed the disturbing news. "Mom, they're suspecting that Dad has had a cerebral hemorrhage," he announced.

Huldah gasped, "Oh, dear God. Is he going to be okay?"

Jim took a hushed breath. "He's in surgery now. We should hear his status shortly."

Huldah felt a cold shudder grip her. She stared numbly at nothing.

Immediately she telephoned Calcutta to talk to the doctors, who assured her the operation was successful and that Mark would fully recover. Though stunned by the grim turn of events, Huldah was relieved and grateful that he was on the mend.

A short time later, like angels of mercy sent from the Throne of God, missionaries Al and Lynette Johnson appeared at the door of her hotel room. When they learned of Mark's condition, they rushed Huldah to the airport to get her airline ticket changed, so she could return to Calcutta to be with Mark. Unfortunately, the first flight available wasn't until the following afternoon.

That night doctors assured Huldah that Mark was responding well to the surgery, so she laid her head down on her pillow confident that she would again look into her husband's eyes. Nonetheless, she tossed in bed most of the night, her heart beating rapidly with worry. Memories of Mark swirled. She replayed their last conversation time and again, searching for any hint that the attack was imminent.

She awoke early the next morning, anticipating a call from Calcutta with the latest prognosis. No call came. She assumed everything was all right and left for the airport with Al Johnson to confirm the change in her ticket.

When they returned to the hotel, Lynette Johnson informed Huldah that she was to return a call from Ron Shaw. He had worked with the Buntains in Calcutta for many years and was now living in the United States.

Ron's voice was noticeably subdued. "Huldah, have you heard from Calcutta?"

"No, not this morning. I've been waiting for a call, but nothing has come through yet."

"Well, when did you talk to Calcutta last?" Ron asked apprehensively.

"Not since last night. I can't understand why they haven't called."

Ron paused. His voice went strangely soft, saying, "Well, the news isn't good. At 8:00 this morning Mark went to be with the Lord."

Huldah stiffened. The terrible pain in her stomach was immediate. In a state of shock, she set the phone down, turned to the Johnsons and asked, "My God, what about the work? What's going to happen to the church and Mission?" She was overcome with visions of a massive ministry without its beloved leader. She could see the long lines of women and children waiting for food, patients streaming into the hospital, children carrying their books to school. Now it all rested on her shoulders.

Without shedding a tear, she began loading her suitcase. "I must get back to Calcutta," she said heavily. "Please, take me to the airport."

Then, stopping to harness her emotions, she burst into uncontrollable tears. "He's gone," she said. "Mark is gone."

The Johnsons put their arms around her and allowed her to cry into their chests.

Flying Home

At the airport, the Johnsons weren't permitted to pass through customs with Huldah. They bid farewell; Huldah was on her own.

Once inside the gate she discovered her plane was facing a two-hour delay. She felt like crying, but there were too many passengers around. She tried to be strong, to wipe the tears as quickly as they came. Finding a place to sit, she began conversing with God in silent prayer.

God, what am I going to do? The work needs Mark.

Somehow she knew heaven was listening.

Lord, this is Your problem. You took Mark home to be with You so suddenly. Now I have to go back to Calcutta and You have to get me someone to help me and be the leader of the people. I don't know what to do.

With her eyes closed, she continued her conversation, as though the Creator were sitting in the chair beside her. *What am I to do?*

Then, an audible voice interrupted her monologue. "Just take it one day at a time."

She awoke from her trance, turning to see which passenger had offered the comforting words.

But there wasn't anyone nearby. *Was it a dream? Where did the voice come from?* she wondered. Somehow she sensed she was experiencing something beyond herself. God was speaking. Clutching onto the armrests, she felt adrenaline flow through her veins like a narcotic.

Tears welled up in her eyes. *I can't,* she told herself. *I mustn't cry here.*

In the distance she could see passengers boarding the plane. She didn't move.

Lord, surely You're not suggesting that I run this ministry without Mark. How is it possible?

Huldah braced herself, uncertain what to do or say next.

Instantly it was as though someone had wrapped a warm blanket around her that brought a calm assurance. "Just take it one day at a time," she repeated softly to herself.

She boarded the plane, still mystified by the miracle of the moment.

Nestling into her seat, she closed her eyes and basked in a generous portion of God's peace.

Arriving in Calcutta

When her plane landed in Calcutta, her meteoric fears began to resurface. She knew a large contingent would be waiting—young and old parishioners anxious to know where she was planning to lead them.

To display their respect for Mark, a row of customs officers lowered their heads as Huldah passed through the gate. A somber-faced soldier snapped to attention, his chest thrust forward, his right hand saluting. Civilians who recognized her were at a loss for words and simply stared away.

Like a scene from a political rally, hundreds of parishioners stood shoulder-to-shoulder in the airport terminal to show their support for Huldah. Hands and arms were extended, wanting to touch her as if she were royalty returning from exile. Tears cascaded down the cheeks of men, women, and children as they expressed their condolences.

Huldah responded courageously. "I know God will help us make it one day at a time," she said. "He will guide us. Mark is in a much better place. He is now with his Savior."

When the crowd began to thin, a staff member said, "Auntie, you must now go and view Pastor's body at the funeral home."

Huldah hesitated, contemplating whether she should refuse. She wanted to remember her husband as he was, not in the form of a frozen corpse. "I'd prefer not to see him like that," she finally confessed.

"Auntie, you must. You will regret it later," one pastor said.

Fear flooded her mind, yet Huldah reluctantly agreed.

For the viewing, Mark's body had to be moved from a freezer to a large table. As Huldah walked into a dilapidated building that the funeral home used for a chapel, fear of the unknown began to trickle down her neck. When her eyes fell on Mark's body, her courage quickly evaporated. *This couldn't be the man I left behind,* she thought, her mouth gaping in horror. Mark's head was bloodstained and heavily bandaged, his eyes closed. His skin was sheet-white, his face puffy and expressionless.

Finally the mad thrashing of her emotions took its toll. She could contain the tears no longer, breaking into deep sobs. Staff members tried to console her, but there was nothing anyone could do to soothe her pain. She had seen an awful sight that would have pierced the most formidable facade.

That night a doctor offered her tablets to help her sleep, but she refused. Thus, sleeping was difficult. Everything from Mark's clothes in the cupboard, to his Bibles on the shelf, to his pictures on the wall reminded her that she would never kiss him again. They would never again share a bed or enjoy an afternoon together with their three grandchildren. Mark had taken many ministry trips and always returned. He had been ill and always recovered. This time it was forever.

Sitting for hours on her verandah, she watched the brilliant sun make its grand entrance and the sky turn blue-green. She exchanged vacant looks with a colony of pigeons and watched a homeless beggar turn in his sleep across the street. Mesmerized by the finality of it all, she gazed out the window, wishing she could summon the audible voice she had heard in the airport.

Suddenly solitude gave way to chaos with a frantic knock at her door and the sound of desperate voices. She quickly strode to see who had intruded on her thoughts.

"You must come to the church immediately," a trusted staff member urged.

"Why?" she responded. "What has happened?"

"There is such a panic with the employees. Many have just now heard about Pastor's passing."

"What? You want me to face the staff today?" she asked with bewilderment. Despair flowed through Huldah's heart again, threatening to engulf her despite the urgency in her assistant's voice. "I can't. Not today. Isn't there someone else who can deal with this?"

"Mrs. Buntain, you're the only one who can calm them and avert a bad situation. There is much at stake."

Huldah's pained expression soon gave way to resignation. She nodded her head in consent. "Yes, I will come right away."

When Mark's death had been announced to the congregation on Sunday, screams were heard echoing throughout the sanctuary and into the streets. Some church members nearly fainted. Now, with word of his death spreading throughout the school and hospital, havoc was breaking out. Employees were reacting to rumors that Mrs. Buntain was leaving Calcutta for good and that she would take some of their jobs with her.

An instant hush fell over the crowd when Huldah stood to address the employees. Many wondered if indeed she would announce her resignation and intention to return to the States. Others wondered if this was the beginning of the end—a church and Mission destined to die without its senior leaders.

Hundreds of dark eyes were fixed on Huldah, employees knowing their futures were hanging in the balance. They waited and hoped.

Though Huldah wasn't feeling brave, she knew if she revealed any sign of weakness it would send the wrong message to the employees. *I need Your help, Father,* she said to herself while stepping to the podium.

Her voice surprisingly forceful, Huldah said, "I'm here. I'm not going anywhere. Be steady, hold on. We will pull this all together. Just continue to do your jobs. Don't worry. God is with us. He will not let us down."

As she uttered these words, the calming effect was immediate. There was a collective sigh of relief among the employees. She wasn't leaving after all. Relieved grins abounded. Their jobs were secure. The fate of the church and Mission was no longer in doubt.

A Special Request

The next few days a stream of visitors came offering their condolences. Among them were city officials. Huldah made it known that she had one request: permission from them to bury Mark where he had planned to build the new sanctuary. He had told her more than once that he wanted to be buried in Calcutta. She determined to do everything in her power to honor his wish.

Some predicted the request would never be approved. Others cautioned that, because of the soil quality, the casket would have to be sealed in a vault. "I believe God will grant my request," Huldah told her aides. "Mark *will* be buried in Calcutta on our property. The Lord will help us."

She spoke with the assurance of one who had received a telegram from God. Indeed, to the surprise of many, the mayor, chief minister, and Christian burial board eventually granted Huldah permission. For her it was another sign that God knew where she was. He knew her needs. And, as long as she took it one day at a time, she could be assured God would bless her.

The funeral procession started at the mortuary and, with hundreds following the hearse, paused at the former church site on Royd Street for government officials to lay wreaths. Store owners pulled down their shades in Mark's honor—an act usually reserved for national officials. Streets were packed with residents and guests from around the world. A large banner was carried behind the hearse, which read: "We love you, Pastor. We will carry on your mission." The hearse then proceeded to Park Street, where Mark's body would be laid to rest.

Twenty thousand had crowded the Park Street complex and streets for the funeral service. Many gathered on the tops of surrounding buildings, where they could be seen weeping and standing at reverent attention. One could almost hear the heavens welcoming this fallen servant to his eternal home.

Surrounded by garlands of flowers, dignitaries took their turn stepping to the microphone to thank God for sending the Buntains to Calcutta. One speaker noted, "Mark lived and walked so closely to God that he was closer to heaven than earth, and so the Lord took him home." There were also testimonies from adults who as children were rescued by Mark from the grips of poverty and disease. Today they serve Jesus Christ as ministers and community leaders.

In Mark's honor, one church member wrote the following for the funeral ceremony:

One man left his mark upon our land. One man who gave God a helping hand. Our founder and our friend, he worked until the end. Today we honor that man. Now that I can go to school I don't feel like such a fool, and it's all because of one man. Clothes to wear, food to eat, I even got shoes upon my feet. It's all because of one man. He saw the need . . . never once worrying what the outcome would be. Such was the bravery of that one man. He looked at the people and saw their need. Children to teach and families to feed so he started working for them. This one man. Schools, a church, and a hospital all built by a man with a dream to fulfill carrying the Lord's own will. This one man. Safe in the arms of Jesus above, he is receiving God's great love. While we pledge to carry on the work of this one man.

Following the funeral service, thousands passed by the missionary's casket in single file, paying their last respects to a spiritual warrior. Some bent to one knee and said a thankful prayer. Most, in silence, closed their eyes and allowed tears to flow. Many recited the words on his gravestone: "A friend of God, he gave of himself for others. He lives on in the hearts of the many he touched. Our precious husband, dad, grampy, and pastor."

The Final Moment

As the casket was being lowered into the black abyss, Huldah felt another eruption of grief and fear. Struck by the finality of the moment, she said to herself, *I can't do this. It's impossible. I just can't do it.* Just as her despair was sinking to new depths, the church's choir stood to sing. The lyrics of their song offered Huldah encouragement: "Were the whole realm of nature mine, that were a present far too small; love so amazing, so divine, demands my soul, my life, my all." To her it spoke of the commitment she owed her Savior. That was a commitment Huldah knew she must cling to, for only in serving God would her heavy burden be lifted.

Then she recited to herself the epitaph that hung above Mark's grave. It was a phrase he often quoted: "Only one prayer I ask, only one good I crave, to finish my task and then to live within an Indian grave."

She thought about other sayings Mark held dear: "My heart is Indian, but my skin is white"; and "Precious India, we are deeply indebted to you. We love you."

Her mind drifted to Proverbs 3:27: "Withhold not good from them to whom it is due, when it is in the power of thine hand to do it" (KJV).

At that moment she knew God was reinforcing His desire for her to stay in Calcutta.

Huldah thought, *Oh God, this is a hard task You're asking me to do. I'm not sure I can do this. Do You really want me to continue leading this work?*

She could almost hear God responding, *I've called you. I will lead you. Just take it one day at a time.*

After the funeral, Huldah retreated to Mark's office. She stopped abruptly at his door. Until now she had not garnered the courage to enter his office. With a deep breath she crossed the threshold. There on Mark's desk lay the architectural drawings for the new sanctuary. As she ran her fingers across the plans, her heart raced with sorrow and emotion at the overwhelming task of completing a building program of this magnitude.

"God, You know I can't build this church," she muttered skeptically. "I don't know one brick from another. What am I going to do? Please tell me, What am I going to do?"

She heard no answer, so she fell limply into Mark's chair and began praying alone.

CHAPTER TWO

A New Leader

B.W. Corpany, executive director of Mission of Mercy, leaned into Mark's office and saw Huldah praying. She lifted her head and their eyes met. As if he could read her consternation, he said, "Huldah, we'll do it. We'll build the church together. I'll help you."

"But who is going to raise the money, B.W.?" she asked, waving her hand for effect.

"God will help us," he replied. "He won't disappoint us. He wants the church built."

B.W. and his wife Carol were deeply devoted to the work. Huldah had often thanked God for sending them to serve with Mission of Mercy. It brought her courage to know she had friends who were so committed to seeing the ministry flourish.

B.W. escorted Huldah to her apartment for lunch, where many out-of-town guests were waiting, engaged in quiet conversation. She tried to appear strong, to hide the relentless pain she was feeling behind her smiling facade. Friends were gracious and supportive, yet Huldah yearned for solitude. Eventually she excused herself from the crowd so she could return to the gravesite and collect some of the flowers. Moreover, she wanted to be alone with her thoughts. She wanted to be alone with Mark just one more time.

The mass of bodies had dispersed by the time Huldah arrived at the grave. There, positioned like a lone sentry, was a gray-haired man, his back slightly humped. His tear-stained, ebony face was unfamiliar to Huldah.

"Did you know him?" she asked.

"Oh, sister, I lost my best friend," he said, not recognizing her as Mark's wife.

"Why do you say that?" she asked, reading foreboding in his eyes.

"No one will help me now," he said, wiping his smudged cheeks.

"What do you mean?"

"This man always put his hand in his pocket and was willing to help me. He was willing to give to the poor. Now nobody will help me."

Even as the stranger spoke, Huldah was seeing flashes of Mark handing food to children and taking an orphan in his arms.

"Sir, he was my husband," she said.

The man lowered his head and cried as though he had lost his brother. "I'm sorry," he said. "I'm so sorry."

"God will help you," Huldah responded. "Follow God. He will help you."

"Yes, thank you," he replied before bowing and walking pensively away.

Huldah wanted to call to the man's back, but she was unable to summon the words.

She stood like a store mannequin for a few moments, gazing absently at Mark's grave. The tears began to resurface as she thought how God had used Mark to touch the lives of so many like this poor man. Many hurting souls would populate heaven because of Mark's obedience and sacrifice.

Mother Teresa

Mother Teresa was not in Calcutta when Mark passed away, but some of her nuns were among those who came to visit Huldah in the days following the funeral. They had depended heavily on Mark and the Mission hospital to treat the destitute and dying from their own mission, so they were anxious to know what would happen to the work now that he was gone.

Mark greatly admired Mother Teresa. Years earlier, he had handwritten a note to his staff that whenever her destitute patients, needy children, or residents needed transportation to the Mission of Mercy hospital, or any other assistance, it was to be provided at no cost.

When Mother Teresa returned to Calcutta, she immediately came to see Huldah and visit Mark's grave. She was greatly moved as she stood with Huldah and read the inscription above the grave. She clutched Huldah's hand, saying, "I will miss him very much. We worked together so well. You must carry on his good work. We must continue loving the poor."

Huldah nodded in agreement.

Mother Teresa then invited Huldah to attend a memorial service to be held in honor of Mark at her mission.

It was a moving memorial service. Huldah sat on the back bench with Mother Teresa, while the nuns sat on the floor. They sang a cappella for half an hour. It sounded like a chorus of angels. A priest offered a beautiful eulogy that lauded Mark's efforts on behalf of the poor, and he thanked God for sending the missionary to help the needy.

Holding Mother Teresa's hand throughout the service, Huldah allowed the tears to stream down her face. She couldn't help but wonder if Mark was listening in. She knew if he could speak to her he would tell her to continue the working relationship with Mother Teresa—a woman who shared his passion to offer hope to the downtrodden.

Mother Teresa later wrote to Huldah, saying:

This brings you my prayers and God's blessing on the wonderful work that has been started by you and Dr. Mark Buntain, and I . . . [want] to show my appreciation. God in His love and tenderness chose you and Dr. Buntain to be His instrument to bring hope, joy, and peace in the lives of many, irrespective of race, caste, and creed. Dr. Buntain's heart was always ready to reach out to the lonely, the sick, the dying, to all those in need of material and spiritual aid. His warm and welcoming smile brought hope in the lives of the poor and rich. He was a man—a doctor, who knew the sacredness of his mission and fulfilled God's will till the end. Taking care of sick Sisters and the poor, he never asked for anything in return but prayer. His selfless, dedicated, sacrificial service has won him an eternal abode of happiness. His presence in all the institutions he founded is still very much alive and is an inspiration to all. May God bless each and everyone who follow his teaching and example and be channels of peace and joy and hope to all. My gratitude to you is my prayer for you.

Electing a Pastor

Jerry Parsley, field secretary for the Assemblies of God, arranged an emergency meeting with the church board and the executive committee of the Assemblies of God of North India. They came together to discuss the selection of a pastor and the future of the church and Mission. They voted unanimously to submit Huldah's name to the congregation as the new senior pastor in the following Sunday morning service. Some years earlier, because she was serving as treasurer of the Assemblies of God of North India, she had been ordained as a minister in India by Field Director Charles Greenaway. Few individuals knew about the ordination because she had placed her certificate in a drawer, where it sat for 19 years. At the time it didn't seem that important. But now she knew why God had made it possible.

After preaching Sunday's message, Jerry Parsley told the congregation that the executive committee and church board were recommending Huldah as the new pastor. Instantly, the congregation began applauding and rose to their feet as one. The applause intensified. Cheers reached a crescendo.

Huldah acknowledged the response with a tearful smile. She motioned for them to be seated, but they ignored her gesture. The clapping continued.

Jerry and Huldah exchanged knowing glances. He said with a grin, "Sister Buntain, I think you've been elected."

The congregation finally returned to their seats and the applause subsided. Huldah accepted the position with a smile and a nod of confidence. For the moment, all was calm. There was no panic. To herself she said, *Don't worry, Huldah, God has everything under control. He knows you can't do this alone.*

Stepping to what was now her pulpit, she started to speak but bowed her head to regain her composure. "I know this is what Mark would have wanted," she finally said. "I miss him as you do, but we must work hard to fulfill his vision. There is much yet to accomplish for God."

The audience again rose to their feet with applause.

When the clapping subsided, she said, "Thank you. I love you. Remain faithful while I am in the States for a brief visit, and when I return we will believe God together that He will continue to work amongst us."

Going Home

The following morning Huldah boarded an airplane with her daughters Maureen and Bonnie to fly to the States. Bonnie's husband Jim was also with them. They were returning to Columbia, Missouri, where a memorial service was scheduled. Memorial services had already been conducted in Tacoma, Colorado Springs, and Edmonton. Another was planned for Vancouver.

For Huldah the memorial service in Columbia was like replaying the funeral in Calcutta all over again:

sympathetic hugs, lengthy tributes, and periods of weeping. Feelings of grief reemerged, and she could not control her saddened expressions. But that wasn't nearly as traumatic as when she pulled into the driveway of their stateside home in Columbia, Missouri. This was where Mark and Huldah had come for rest and study while itinerating in the States. The triplex, the only home they ever owned, represented many fond memories.

"Are you sure you don't want to just come home with Bonnie and me?" Jim asked, his finger on the garage door opener.

"Jim, if I don't sleep in that bed tonight and get our things packed, I won't be able to move on with life," she said.

Huldah opened the front door with trepidation, her first step inside tentative. She studied the family photos on the wall and the furniture as if they were part of an art exhibit. Mark had come home in March to receive the prestigious Helping Hands Award from World Relief, so there was still food in the refrigerator and clothes in the closet. Memories were everywhere. Many more were downstairs in Mark's office. She tried to muster the courage to descend the menacing stairs, but she could not. That would have to wait until morning. She crawled into bed and sorted through a pile of telegrams and letters from loyal friends and fans:

Dear Huldah:

You can be assured of my prayers. India will miss Pastor Buntain and the unselfish service he gave to the poor and needy in its desperate streets. It all feels like a bad dream. As Christians we have hope for the future that one day we will be reunited with our loved ones. Our Father in heaven called Pastor to retire from his mission on earth and I can imagine Pastor saying, "Oh Lamb of God, I come." If there is anything I can do for you, please let me know.

Dear Huldah:

This is to let you know we are standing with you at this time. You and Mark have always had a special place in our hearts. I've often told people that Mark was the greatest example of being a missionary that I had ever met. He certainly ran the race before him. So many are going to miss him, perhaps most of all, the city of Calcutta. Surely he gained for heaven many thousands of souls. What was said of King David can surely be said of Brother Mark: "For David after he had served his own generation by the will of God fell on to sleep." Surely the Lord will stand with you.

I know from experience that even though we know our loved ones are safe in the arms of our Lord, it is an overwhelming experience to adjust to their absence in our daily lives. Brother Buntain had a direct hand in my salvation, as it was soon after he visited our church that I was saved. I was so impressed with his devotion to the work he is doing, he became my first missionary supportee. I know there are millions of us who are feeling his loss.

Dear Huldah:

No one person could possibly put into words what your dear heart is feeling. Yet, thank the Lord, God knows exactly what you are feeling and He is ever in your presence. I have always looked to you as a mentor. To me you have become the perfect example of a missionary's wife. Pastor Buntain said that his dear Huldah was the foundation and strength of the work in Calcutta. I wish I could say the perfect words that would heal the loneliness and sorrow you must feel. I just know God still has beautiful things planned for your life. You are truly anointed.

One letter read: "Huldah, we will pray for you as you consider whether you should now live in the United States." That message made her stop and think of all that she would miss by returning to India. It wouldn't be easy for her or her family. Huldah's love for her three grandchildren, two daughters, and son-in-law made leaving the States and returning to Calcutta difficult. She treasured the opportunities to play with the children and shop with Bonnie and Maureen. She enjoyed visiting with Jim at the dinner table. She wanted to be near her sister Beulah. Still, Huldah knew, for now, her place was in Calcutta. Many friends and staff members were anxiously awaiting her return, longing for her leadership as administrator *and* pastor.

But that did not make the flight back any easier. As the jet pierced a layer of clouds, she couldn't help but feel she was flying into a dark void filled with uncertainty. She peered out the window at the billowing clouds, though watching more with her mind than her eyes. She tried to force anticipation and confidence to the surface of her emotions, but they were smothered by discouragement and feelings of inadequacy. Separation from her family and the monumental task before her also shrouded her sense of contentment.

Before the hum of the jetliner could cast her into a slumber, she prayed, *Dear God, I have never pastored a church and the challenge of the other ministries is so great. You are my only hope.*

Again, she felt God's presence and a dose of courage that only He can give. Without worry, she fell asleep.

Fortunately, she had no idea what awaited her in Calcutta. Otherwise, she would have been too nervous to even close her eyes.

CHAPTER THREE

The Battles

Huldah was met at Calcutta's airport with some alarming news. It had been widely publicized that she would be preaching the following morning in the Sunday service. She had spoken at women's functions, missions conventions, and seminars, but a Sunday morning service was a proposition she found frightening. Fears were compounded when she learned it would be a joint service, with all eight language congregations that made up the main Assemblies of God church in Calcutta.

She didn't even have a sermon she could pull from a file, so that evening Huldah stayed awake well past midnight preparing and praying. She told herself there was nothing to fear. She was now the senior pastor, she recited to herself, and she had to take charge. She couldn't let anyone know she was scared. There couldn't be a shred of fear in her voice or a bead of perspiration on her forehead.

Secretly she feared that church attendance might begin to decline because she was not a revered preacher like Mark. Then there were the unfamiliar functions such as conducting her first wedding and funeral services. She wasn't a trained counselor or theologian. She was an experienced pastor's wife, gifted administrator, and student of the Bible. But she wondered if that was enough.

When she walked onto the platform to speak, she thought, *What am I doing here? I shouldn't be here. I'm only the wife of Mark Buntain. I sit behind a desk. I'm not a pastor.*

Using an interpreter—which gave her a chance to collect her thoughts between sentences—she preached a message entitled "Carrying On." Throughout her message her eyes scanned the capacity crowd for a hint of dissatisfaction—a sign that boredom had set in. To her delight, it was soon obvious she had earned the attention of both familiar faces and complete strangers. With the anointing of the Holy Spirit, her words had come alive. Young people were sitting on the edge of their seats. Adults had tears in their eyes. And when she issued the altar call, young and old alike pressed forward. The experience reminded her of God's words to her: As long as she focused on the duties of today, her Creator would carry her through challenging days just like this one.

New Challenges

Suddenly she had assumed the role of senior pastor, director of Calcutta Mission of Mercy, president of West Bengal Bible College, and a leader in the Assemblies of God of North India. Mark had always maintained that his wife possessed the gifts and ability to run General Motors; now she would have the chance to prove he was right.

Unfortunately, the challenges didn't wait for her to settle into her post. Soon after taking the reins, she faced many difficulties, but she was thankful to God for giving her wisdom and guidance. She was warned that many similar organizations were facing strikes and staff problems. Because of the great respect workers had for Mark and appreciation for the sacrifices he had made through the years, she was certain she could weather the storms which could arise among 1,500 employees. She was confident God would help her navigate through turbulent waters.

Huldah was heard saying many times, "If God be for us, who can stand against us?" Although she knew the enemy would do all he could to destroy the work, she believed the God who had led Mark would also guide her.

Reliance on God was her only answer. She had worked alongside Mark in administration and finances, but she was now facing imposing, unfamiliar responsibilities. Many nights, leaving the office late, she put her key into the door and said a prayer: "God, this is the one day that You promised to help me with and I have done my best, so I must leave today with You and take up the responsibility again tomorrow morning."

And when morning came and her key reentered the lock, she prayed: "God, this is the day You promised me. I am taking it one day at a time as You told me to do. Please help me again today."

When others applauded her stamina, strength, and ability, she was quick to give God the credit. She knew it was only the leading of the Holy Spirit that helped her not be intimidated by the task at hand.

Riots in the Streets

When fighting broke out in North India between religious factions, the entire city was ordered under curfew for one week. At night especially, the city's normally chaotic streets became empty and eerily quiet. Tensions were high; any false move among civilians could have severe consequences. With food running short at the boys' home, hospital, senior citizens home, and at the Mission—where nursing school and college students lived—Huldah devised a plan to resolve the situation. With the help of the hospital staff, she dispatched their ambulance—which was authorized to be on the streets—to gather food and deliver it to the respective institutions. To the young and elderly alike she was an instant heroine. But there were more challenges ahead that weren't so easily solved.

One night, without a star in sight and the air unusually damp, the religious war escalated and spread to Calcutta's streets. Some women and children raced into the Mission's School of Nursing hostel to find sanctuary. The mob wouldn't be deterred. They ran up and down Park Street, passing the Mission complex. A smattering of stones shattered the windows of the Mission. The rioters shook their fists and shouted obscenities. The attack sent some construction workers fleeing the compound.

Huldah remained unruffled by the conflict. She called her daughters in the States and described the crisis to them with the calm assurance of a veteran who had seen it all before. She had experienced two wars, blackouts, riots, and many other problems. This was nothing new. Yet, she never took God's faithfulness for granted. She knew the power of prayer during situations such as this. On many occasions she and Mark had dropped everything to pray for God's help during a crisis.

Devastating Fire

It was 4 a.m. when the phone rang beside Huldah's bed. A fire had broken out in the slum area behind the Mission. Huldah quickly dressed and ran downstairs to a car that had been sent for her. Billows of smoke and flames soared. Some members of the staff beat a quick path to help fight the spreading blaze, which was appearing more hopeless with each minute. The fire trucks arrived but there was no water, no hydrants. "God help us," Huldah prayed as the fire was moving toward the Mission. Suddenly she remembered that Mark had ordered the installation of a water system underneath the Mission complex. The fire chief was informed of the reservoir and his hoses were dropped into the hole. Moments later water was spraying toward the flames, which had already enveloped a portion of the vocational school. It was apparent that without divine intervention the Mission buildings would become a heap of ashes.

It took hours for the firefighting crew and local volunteers to control the fire. Almost as though God had imposed an invisible fire wall, flames stopped short of the main school building. Hundreds looked on with astonishment that the tall flames had not spread to the other buildings. It was another example of God's protective power.

The newspaper declared in its headline: "250 shops and many dwellings completely gutted in devastating blaze, 150 flee to safety; flames threaten nearby Mission and Hospital." Fire officials said if it hadn't been for the Mission's water reservoir, the Mark Buntain Education Center would have burned to the ground. Surely God had led Mark, years earlier, to install the reservoir. Because of that decision, the Mission and hospital were spared the fate of other buildings that burned to the ground.

The Ambulance and Freezer

It was the heart of the summer. The city was experiencing high temperatures—even for Calcutta. Children jostled for a chance to dip their heads in a bucket of water. Barefoot rickshaw pullers continued to work, despite their blistering feet, so they could feed their families.

Huldah was at her desk, and it was as hot as any time she could remember. She received a call from the hospital that there had been a death and the local mortuary's freezer had broken down. This was a common occurrence, so the medical director reminded Huldah that the hospital needed its own freezer. A week earlier, in a committee meeting, the need was discussed along with the need for an ambulance that was small enough to negotiate Calcutta's narrow lanes.

For Huldah it was another test. There were so many projects for which to raise funds. Would she have the faith? "I believe God will meet our need if everyone will pray," she said, challenging the pastors to fast and intercede on their knees.

Once again God heard her cry. From an unlikely source, an offering arrived to pay for the ambulance and freezer. What an encouragement it was to the staff, and a reminder that the miracles did not die with Pastor Mark Buntain. God was still present and prepared to display His power through those who sought His face.

Shortage of Funds

Whenever funds ran low and the Mission didn't have money to purchase food for the feeding lines—which thousands depended on for survival—Huldah would remind God of an incident during the early days of the feeding program: Mark was summoned to the accounts office to learn there was no money to buy the next day's food. That day Mark held hands with the accountant and Huldah and prayed a few short sentences. "God, You know this need," he said. "The children need food. I believe You will supply the funds so we can feed these poor ones tomorrow." Within a few hours Mark returned to the accounts office waving an envelope containing $1,000. With a wide smile he said, "Didn't I tell you God would provide?"

This scene was repeated time and again through the years. And in each instance God sent the financial miracle they needed.

But now there was no Mark. Huldah knew she must have the same faith to believe God for miracles. As the days passed, it was obvious God was honoring Huldah's leadership and faith by supplying the funds needed for the monumental task before her and her congregation.

A New Schedule

Not long before Mark's passing, he came home after a Wednesday night service terribly discouraged. "I just don't know why more people aren't coming out for midweek service," he said.

Huldah tried to offer an explanation. "I think it is the wrong night. You know how difficult the educational program is here, and how the children have so much homework. And with the compulsory language courses many have to take private tutoring in the evenings and parents have to sit long hours with their children."

"Yes," Mark said, "I think you're right. Is there anything we can do?"

"I think we should have a family night on Fridays. Saturday is a holiday and the children can do their lessons then. That will allow families to attend. And let's have something for every age group."

Mark smiled with renewed enthusiasm. "That's an excellent idea. Let's go to work on it right away."

Mark passed away before the new schedule could be implemented. But Huldah revived the project, telling the people it was Mark's wishes. Soon momentum swelled in all eight language sections. Friday nights became an integral part of the church, offering services for every age group. The innovation was praised by many, and once again Huldah's leadership proved to be Spirit-led. So, when she suggested that home fellowship groups, extension Bible schools, city branch churches, and more outstation works be developed, everyone had confidence these programs would be successful. And they were.

Loneliness

Despite her successes, Huldah occasionally found herself battling loneliness. She had learned to bury her emotions in her work, but on many occasions—especially holidays when the office was closed—she would feel that emptiness. When couples her age would visit, she would be reminded of her close relationship with Mark. She would ask, "Why me, God? Why did I have to be left alone?" Often her mind would be preoccupied with memories of her special times with Mark: their prayers at the breakfast table, the intimate discussions, visits with parishioners, prayers for the sick, and when they traveled from one church to another to share their vision. The memories were soothing, but the reality of his absence often only provoked heartache.

Whenever obstacles appeared invincible or she was afflicted with bouts of loneliness, Huldah opened her *Living Bible*. So many times Scriptures had provided the comforting words she needed. Many years before, she had learned to cope with separation from Mark. She had grown accustomed to his fund-raising and preaching tours. But these days the loneliness was of a different sort. Mark was gone forever and her period of mourning lingered like an unforgettable nightmare. Not since the time she experienced the death of her second child, had Huldah endured such inner pain. For that reason, she found herself spending more and more time in her work and praying that God would help her with the many dreams and visions Mark had for the Mission.

Huldah was well aware that the enemy would attempt to dismantle the ministry God had built. He would attack on every front. But, ultimately, Huldah knew the future of the Mission and the destiny of thousands rested on her intimacy and dependence upon her heavenly Father. As long as she stayed close to God, there was nothing to fear. Many times in prayer she would remind God of His promise to her in the Bangkok airport: *Take it one day at a time and I will help you.* And each time she felt the assurance of His presence.

CHAPTER FOUR

A Shrine to God

"I think the call of God comes to people in different ways," Huldah said in an interview with evangelist Rich Wilkerson. "When I came here and saw such need, it immediately made me know God had brought me here for a purpose. To get your heart and soul into the work, you have to feel God has brought you. When we stepped off the boat many years ago, I was struck by the children of Calcutta, the poverty—and I just couldn't stand by and do nothing about it. To me that is a divine calling."

It was her calling that had sustained her during Mark's illnesses, his absences from home, and the many trials; and it was that calling and the Word of God that would have to sustain her now. She often gathered strength from the Book of Esther, which relates five steps Queen Esther took to accept change: she asked God for courage, strength, determination, dedication, and commitment. When Esther was confronted with challenges, she wasn't sure she possessed these traits. So she petitioned God for help. Likewise, Huldah found herself asking God to provide what she lacked in the face of her challenges. She was being asked to complete the construction of the new sanctuary, to find dormitories for the nurses' school, to launch a cardiac unit in the hospital, and more. "I do not have the expertise to meet these demands," she prayed time and again, "so I ask You, Father, to do for me what You did for Esther. Grant me the courage, strength, determination, dedication, and commitment to complete Your work." With God's help, Huldah vowed to press on. She prayed, she planned, she acted.

Building a Church

Building permits for new churches were not being issued in Calcutta. The church on Royd Street was the first Christian church built in the city in more than a century. Believing that somehow God would provide the permit, Mark had moved forward with architectural drawings for the new sanctuary.

Days before Mark's passing, he and the architect had altered the building plans. They had decided to put the Bible college on the lower floor of the church building. This change made it necessary for Huldah to submit a new set of drawings to the appropriate officials. She needed their approval in the form of a building permit before she could erect the magnificent building.

The fulfillment of Mark's vision rested in Huldah's lap. She wasn't sure what to do. Mark had always coordinated the building projects. Now the congregation and staff were looking to her to guide them through the process.

Some felt the building plans would never be approved, but Huldah persevered as if she were a modern-day Noah. Skeptics thought her notion to build such an enormous facility in downtown Calcutta was impossible. Their unbelief left Huldah unswayed. After all, this wasn't her project or Mark's; this building belonged to God. She believed He would provide the permits needed, and there was nothing the forces of darkness could do to prevent it. "He hasn't brought us this far to retreat," she told the congregation, referring to how God had miraculously provided the property on Park Street many years earlier.

The land was originally a nineteenth-century British cemetery, which had dissuaded Hindus and Muslims from submitting a bid for the property. Thus, Mark had been afforded the chance to obtain the property on a long-term renewable lease. His battles were not over, however, as a portion of the property was occupied by squatters who had built hovels on the land. Construction couldn't commence until they had vacated the premises. According to Indian custom, it would take an act of God to remove them from their makeshift homes. Mark prayed by the hour in his office. He sent letters to his friends in the States and Canada, asking them to pray. He needed to touch heaven.

One morning God answered his prayers by allowing a fire to break out on the property. The squatters fled the flames and never returned.

More obstacles were ahead, however. As the foundation for the hospital was being dug, the hole filled with water seeping from an underground reservoir. Within hours, it looked more like a swimming pool than a foundation. Mark beckoned the employees to gather around the hole and pray for victory. He pulled a small Bible from his pocket and put it into a cement box. They prayed and then the box was lowered into the water. Mark gave the order for the workmen to start pouring the gravel into the foundation. To herself that day Huldah prayed, *God, please help us. Mark has worked so hard, and we've gotten so close to seeing this hospital built. Please don't let this discourage him. Give him the faith he needs to see Your work carried on.* Shortly thereafter, the seepage stopped in miraculous fashion and building commenced on schedule. Even when the hospital was built and rains caused extensive flooding in surrounding buildings, the hospital basement remained dry.

Now, some years later, Huldah and her congregation were in need of another miracle. The congregation fasted and prayed that the building permit would be issued, for without God's help the vision for a new sanctuary would evaporate as quickly as the water that once filled the foundation.

Huldah, day after day, awoke early and rode to the office. Before the staff arrived, she sat in silent stillness behind her desk and asked God to make a way for the construction of the church to proceed.

One day Huldah was informed the building inspector was coming to her office. She didn't know if he was coming to deny her permit, or if he was going to impose a sanction of some kind. Nervously she prayed for God's help while the official marched toward her office.

Huldah explained her problems to the inspector. He listened respectfully. Unbeknownst to Huldah, her decision to bury Mark in Calcutta was comparable to a written decree that he had adopted India as his homeland. The inspector was noticeably impressed that Mark had been buried on the church premises and the building was to be known as the Mark Buntain Memorial Assemblies of God Church.

"How long have you been in India?" he asked.

"Nearly 40 years," Huldah replied.

He smiled. "You've been here longer than I have been alive."

Huldah nodded.

He then informed her of his decision to approve the new plans.

Once again God was faithful. In a grand celebration, with hundreds of parishioners looking on, the cornerstone was laid. That day Huldah had a sense Mark had a bird's-eye view of the ceremony. At least she hoped he could see the fruit of his labor. His vision was finally coming to pass.

Huldah understood, however, it was one thing to lay a cornerstone and quite another to complete the project. The foreboding task of raising the funds to erect such a magnificent structure still remained.

Raising the Funds

Huldah laid plans to return to the States and Canada to share with congregations her burden for the lost and hurting of Calcutta and to solicit financial assistance to build the sanctuary.

For many years she and Mark had traveled from church to church as young evangelists in North America. They had many memorable experiences during their services: a woman was healed of scarlet fever; an ominous, destructive storm bypassed a farmer's crops; a truck driver was miraculously converted. There were also many personal experiences: Mark was healed of a life-threatening allergic reaction; he was rescued from a near-drowning fishing incident; the endless days on the road; and long nights in dilapidated evangelist quarters and humble motels. But it was in these valuable early years, in mostly smaller churches, that Mark honed his preaching skills.

Once they had served a term in Calcutta, Mark was in high demand as a speaker. Pastors of the largest churches in the States and Canada were calling to have Mark stand in their pulpit. He had developed a reputation as a pulpiteer and masterful fund-raiser. Congregations responded to his sincerity and passion; they were moved by stories of desperate children who were given hope. His missions services and altar calls were legendary.

Now it was yet to be seen whether Huldah could be as successful. This tour would take her to large congregations from coast to coast. People would travel long distances to hear her tell missionary stories and preach. Churches would invest in newspaper ads and flyers, inviting people to attend her special services. Huldah secretly wondered if she possessed the speaking ability to meet their high expectations. And the challenge of inspiring audiences to give generously to the new sanctuary project filled her with further trepidation.

She prayed alone in her hotel room before services, asking God to stir hearts: "Lord, make this more than a fund-raising service. Touch lives. Give me the boldness to speak Your Word forcefully."

One of her messages centered on Luke 10 and the story of the Good Samaritan: "A man fell upon thieves and was lying in a ditch. We see this very image in Calcutta's streets. A complete stranger lifted him from the ditch and took him to an inn, and he told the innkeeper, 'Whatsoever thou spendest more, I will repay you when I come.' It's that 'more' that moves the heart of God. When we give sacrificial offerings and of ourselves, it moves God," she preached.

Huldah was delighted and relieved when crowds responded enthusiastically to her messages. It thrilled her to see young people being called to the ministry and adults accepting Christ for the first time. Praying with them at the altar and encouraging future missionaries was as fulfilling as anything she had ever experienced.

Her smile was a portrait of gratitude when she watched children give their last dollar, senior citizens on fixed incomes make pledges, and churches empty their missions accounts to reach out to the people of Calcutta. Because of the generosity of God's people, Huldah was able to return to Calcutta with the funds to underwrite the building project.

Not Enough

Some months passed and construction was in full swing. Craftsmen and laborers were everywhere. Scaffolding bracketed the outer walls of the facility. Anticipation was growing. Then Huldah received disheartening news. She sat in disbelief when she learned the rising costs of building materials had far exceeded projected estimates. The funds she had raised were now insufficient. The building fund account was empty.

One day a contractor came to Huldah's office expecting to be paid.

Huldah responded, "I'm sorry, God hasn't sent it yet."

The man left without complaint, though Huldah worried he might pull his crew off the project. Later that day he poked his head into Huldah's office, asking, "Did *He* send it yet?"

"Not yet," Huldah answered, "but it is on its way."

A few days later, the contractor returned. "Is it here yet?" he asked, with a trace of frustration.

With a grin, Huldah said, "Yes, sir, He *has* sent it. You can pick up your check at 3:00."

Halfway through the building project another crisis materialized. Huldah had hoped to construct the church in granite to avoid the high cost of painting the building year after year, as she had experienced with other buildings in the complex. One day an exasperated contractor plopped into a chair in Huldah's office, claiming it was impossible to get any more granite from Bangalore in South India.

Huldah knew if they could not get granite the dedication celebration that was scheduled for January would be in jeopardy. She begged him to do his best, saying, "We can't delay the dedication."

She knew that postponement was not an option. More than 50 people from the States and Canada had already purchased their airline tickets and adjusted their work schedules. *What an embarrassment it would be for guests to arrive to dedicate an incomplete sanctuary*, she thought.

One night she sat on the edge of her bed and talked to God: "Dear Lord, we have to complete the church on time. I've done all I know to do. You've helped me this far. Please help me again. Please give me direction."

She reached for her *Living Bible*, where she often found encouragement during a crisis. She prayed, "God, give me the right verses that I need." She opened her Bible to 1 Chronicles 28:19,20: "Be strong and courageous and get to work. Don't be frightened by the size of the task, for the Lord my God is with you; he will not forsake you. He will see to it that everything is *finished correctly*."

She promptly wrote in the margin of her Bible, "New church—answered prayer."

A few weeks passed, and there was still no granite and no hope in sight. Huldah kept believing God for a miracle. Then the promise Huldah received from God was validated. Granite was suddenly available, and it would be sent in a few days. Construction would proceed on schedule. The dedication service would be saved.

Other miracles helped bring the building to completion. A year before Mark's death, he met a couple who owned a large tannery that exported leather to Western countries. Their daughter was dying of leukemia. Mark visited their home frequently and, when she was brought to the Mission hospital, he was with the family constantly. Although their daughter passed away, the parents were so moved by Mark's love and concern that they gave their hearts to the Lord and became faithful members of the church.

In the years following God blessed their business. While other tanneries were having difficulty exporting leather, their business flourished. To express their gratitude to God and the church, they donated all the leather for the pews in the new sanctuary.

There were many people in the congregation who gave sacrificially so the church could be built. Some worked second jobs; others donated family heirlooms and what little savings they had. One woman, a retired schoolteacher, asked her former principal if she could have a small snack bar for the students. When he asked her why, she said, "I do not have money to help build my dear pastor's church, and this way I can give my share to help with the construction." Once she had his permission, she worked day after day making snacks to be sold to the students. Each month she brought the profits to Huldah to be deposited in the building fund.

Together they were building a monument to God, and no price was too great. The church's large cross, just above Mark's grave, would rise above the city—a symbol of God's superiority in the needy city of Calcutta—a billboard to tell hurting people that Jesus is the answer.

Dedication Service

When guests arrived at their hotel they were unaware that a crew was working feverishly to have the building completed for the dedication ceremony scheduled for the following day. Huldah made her way to the sanctuary to inspect their progress. Her daughter Bonnie advised her not to go inside. "Don't go in, Mother. It will upset you. Don't worry, it will all be ready by tomorrow."

Reading the consternation in Bonnie's face, Huldah said, "I don't think it will be ready tomorrow."

The contractor overheard Huldah's comment. "Mrs. Buntain," he said, "go home and rest. Come back tomorrow morning and you will see everything will be finished correctly."

She couldn't believe her ears. The non-Christian contractor had repeated the last two words from the passage Huldah had read in First Chronicles of the *Living Bible*. Huldah and Bonnie went home believing the sanctuary would be completed as promised.

The next morning Huldah was filled with gratitude as she walked into the sanctuary. Workmen had labored through the night to finish their task. One only needed to look into Huldah's glistening eyes to know she was pleased with the craftsmanship. She thought, *It is true, dear God, You will never leave us or forsake us. You have made this possible, and we give You all the glory.*

January 24, 1993, the dedication was held. The balconies were overflowing; the sanctuary floor was without an empty seat, forcing people to listen from the lobby. G. Raymond Carlson, then general superintendent of the Assemblies of God, preached the dedication service, saying, "I believe Mark is looking down on us today. Mark was an unusual man. I counted him as a friend since the days of our youth in 1934, when I attended his father's Bible school in Canada. Mark never changed in his commitment to God. He was possessed with a burning desire to please his Lord. His passion for his beloved India fairly consumed him. Eternity alone will reveal the ingathering of harvest garnered through his tears, his preaching, his loving, and his care for the multitudes. Who can measure the impact which his wife Huldah had upon Mark's ministry? What a great team."

Huldah followed, saying to the vast congregation, "Let us today, together, rededicate ourselves to carry out the vision that Pastor had . . . to press on regardless of difficulties and to continue the mission and work that God accomplished through him."

She continued by declaring her firm belief that the words on Mark's grave were true: "He lives on in the lives he touched . . . and trained."

The smiling crowd glowed with anticipation, knowing the Mission's greatest days were ahead.

The Cardiac Unit

The following day, an addition to the hospital was also dedicated: the Mark Buntain Cardiac Unit. This was a vision Mark and Jim, his son-in-law, shared. Jim was now a thoracic surgeon heading the artificial heart program in Salt Lake City. It would be a unit complete with heart specialists and the latest diagnostic equipment. But, months earlier, space limitations had threatened to delay the project. The fifth floor of the hospital—the ideal location for the unit—was being used as a dormitory for the student nurses. The floor had to be vacated before the unit could be installed. Huldah's search for alternative housing for the students had proven unsuccessful. For months she had pursued one lead after another, growing weary of dead ends and agreements gone awry. When there *was* space available, owners were reluctant to lease it for that purpose. Huldah knew the importance of the unit and she couldn't tolerate a delay. The hospital staff was having to refer patients complaining of chest pains to other hospitals. But the poor couldn't afford the costly treatment in other hospitals, so they often lived in pain.

One day, Huldah heard about a building being constructed across from the hospital. It was an ideal location for the students' hostel. She contacted the owner and made arrangements to inspect the facility. While touring the apartments, Huldah's eyes were wide with enthusiasm. She felt this was God's provision, although she didn't know where the money for the building would come from. She just knew God would provide. "Yes, we'll take it," she said.

Next, Huldah had to gather medical equipment to furnish the cardiac unit. Purchasing the equipment was too costly. Huldah had no alternative but to ask God for another miracle.

Tears filled her eyes as she was talking to Bob Pagett of Assist International. "I will help you get the equipment you need," he said. A few days later, she talked with Dave Harrington of American Medical Resources Foundation, who also offered his help. Together they gathered the equipment needed to furnish the cardiac unit.

Another challenge remained: the shipping and delivery of the equipment. At the time, the Mission had not yet been included in the Indo-U.S. Bilateral Agreement, which would simplify future shipments of medical supplies and equipment. Huldah also knew the duty fees would be costly, which she could not afford.

Huldah contacted Mother Teresa's private physician, who had become a good friend of Jim Long and the Mission. The doctor and Huldah paid a visit to Mother Teresa to explain how the unit would save many lives and request her help in getting the equipment delivered.

Mother Teresa understood the need for the unit, for she had also found it difficult to obtain cardiac care for her patients. She became involved in the negotiations. Because of her participation and interest, officials assisted in getting the equipment delivered on time and at no cost to the hospital.

For Huldah, the entire episode was a test of faith. Bob Pagett, Dave Harrington, and a group of engineers arrived at the hospital to install the equipment. They were on a tight schedule and had to complete the installation in several days. But the equipment still had not arrived. To stall for time, Huldah took the men on a lengthy tour, praying with each step the truck containing the equipment would reach its destination. She didn't know what to tell the men. They had traveled so far to complete the project. She prayed silently, *Lord, what should I do? We're running out of time. If it doesn't arrive soon, it will be a wasted trip for them.*

In faith, she said, "Gentlemen, why don't you go to the hotel, get cleaned up from your long trip, and come back later this evening to install the equipment."

But as they descended the stairs to the ground floor, their eyes fell on the truck carrying the equipment.

"There it is now," Huldah exclaimed. "It has come just in time. God has timed it just right."

The men didn't go to the hotel, instead choosing to begin installing the equipment immediately.

Jim was beaming with excitement the day of the dedication, knowing the dream had been fulfilled. Mark's brother Fulton was also on hand to lead the ceremony. He assisted Mother Teresa in cutting the ceremonial ribbon. Mother Teresa said, "This will be used as a place of service for the poor and needy in this city of Calcutta."

And how right she was.

CHAPTER FIVE

The World Traveler

The demand for Huldah to speak at missions conventions and churches around the world continued to increase. When on tour, she found herself boarding airplanes day after day to raise funds necessary to propel the Mission, Bible college, and village churches. On one flight, from Massachusetts to Salt Lake City, the captain's voice came over the loudspeaker: "We are having some mechanical difficulties caused by an oil leak. Please keep your seatbelts fastened. No meals will be served. We will be flying low and plan to force-land in St. Louis to switch planes."

Some passengers were terrified. The young man sitting beside Huldah stuttered, "Oh, this is terrible. Just terrible."

"Don't worry, sir," Huldah said with a resigned shrug. "It won't crash."

"How do you know?" he exclaimed, his arms folded.

"I know because God looks after me. And my work isn't finished."

Looking at Huldah with a peculiar expression, the man muttered under his breath, "I wish I could be so sure."

Huldah smiled. "Oh, you can." She proceeded to share with him her life and the plan of salvation. His interest in Jesus began peaking as the plane approached the tarmac.

But when the plane touched down safely, and waiting fire engines and ambulances weren't necessary, the young man's interest quickly waned. Huldah thought, *So many want God's help, but they don't want to fully serve Him. Father, help me to continue trusting You and serving You no matter what circumstances I face.*

700 Club

Terry Meeuwsen, cohost of television's *700 Club*, visited Calcutta to do some filming and present a check for $10,000 to Huldah for the Mission. During that visit, Terry invited Huldah to appear on the program.

On her next tour of the States, Huldah flew to Virginia Beach to the studios of Christian Broadcasting Network. Knowing hundreds of thousands were watching her interview didn't seem to concern Huldah. She conversed as if visiting over a cup of tea at her dining table—oblivious to the stage lights, camera crew, and TelePrompTers. She spoke confidently about what God was accomplishing in Calcutta.

"This whole work is a miracle," Terry responded. "But after Mark's passing it would have been easy to say you'd put many years in and now it was time to go home to the United States and put your feet up in an easy chair. Why did you stay?"

Huldah replied, "I found the notes to the last message Mark was preparing to preach. He had highlighted the words, 'I gave, I gave my life for thee; what hast thou given for me?' It reminded me that no commitment was too large. But, quite honestly, there *was* a temptation to leave. I had been there for 35 years; but how could I leave without finishing the projects Mark had started? I just knew God wanted me there."

Phone banks lit up during the program as callers sought additional information about the work in Calcutta. Many asked for a copy of Huldah's biography, *Treasures in Heaven.* They wanted to know more about this woman who had given the best years of her life to the people of Calcutta.

Honorary Doctorate

Huldah received a letter from the president of North Central Bible College in Minneapolis, Minnesota, indicating the institution's desire to present her with an honorary doctorate.

Embedded in Huldah's memory was the night Mark was awarded an honorary doctorate from the University of Missouri. It astounded her to think she would be considered for a similar honor.

The auditorium at North Central Bible College was filled to capacity. Many had come just to hear Huldah expound on the components of a successful missionary. From the podium, Huldah gazed at her youthful audience. It seemed like only yesterday when she was young too. She had learned many important principles about life and ministry through the years, and this was a cherished opportunity to share with those who would one day follow in her footsteps. She wanted them to know that success should not be their goal in life; they should strive to be faithful to God. They shouldn't seek personal glory; they should seek to give God glory.

At the conclusion of her speech, students responded with a standing ovation. They had heard from a veteran missionary advocating proven principles. For young men and women she was a role model, an example of what God can accomplish through the life of a committed servant. Her life was a symbol of courage, sacrifice, and perseverance. One student, as he left the auditorium, summed up the feelings of many: "Dr. Huldah Buntain represents everything the world preaches against. She chose obscurity over fame, sacrifice over security, spiritual character over comfort."

Hearing the Holy Spirit

As Huldah was preaching at Orlando Christian Center in Florida, she was unaware what was occurring in Pastor Benny Hinn's heart. He sat behind her on the platform and cried throughout her message. The Holy Spirit, that morning, spoke to him that he was to help Huldah. He was to visit her in Calcutta.

Some months later, the Mission found itself in desperate need of funds. Huldah gathered the staff for an impromptu prayer meeting. "We need a miracle," she said. "This is serious. Pray like you have never prayed before." The men and women held hands, each petitioning heaven with the urgency of a death-bed prayer.

"I believe God has heard our prayer today," a pastor commented.

"Amen," said another.

"God is going to meet our need," one echoed.

It blessed Huldah to see the youthful staff members claiming God's provision so boldly. Their faith was maturing. *Mark would be so proud of the way they are following in his footsteps of faith,* she thought.

Their faith would mushroom and be rewarded when Benny Hinn made the epic flight to Calcutta.

Not only would Benny bless the Mission and hospital, he would also have an unforgettable spiritual experience in Calcutta. Riding into town from the airport, he was struck by the squalid poverty and desolation. He spotted a woman holding a baby in threadbare clothing; she was staring hopelessly at a wall. He held a handkerchief to his nose to block the awful stench, and he closed his eyes to escape the despair. Nothing had prepared him for what he saw.

Benny followed Huldah through the streets and hospital corridors. He was moved to tears as he walked through a maze of cribs in the pediatric ward. It suddenly struck him that many of these children would be dead if it weren't for the Mission.

"I'm here," he said to Huldah, "because on the platform when you spoke the Holy Spirit said to me, *If you will help the poor, I will never cease to bless what you're doing.* I'm here because God commanded me to be a blessing to you. Mrs. Buntain, this is for your work here."

He presented Huldah with a donation of $75,000.

Huldah tearfully thanked Benny and could hardly wait to spread the news of God's provision to her praying staff members. Once again God had proven His faithfulness.

General Council

At the General Council of the Assemblies of God in Portland, Oregon, Huldah was the guest speaker at

The church in Calcutta rejoiced for answered prayer.

Even with treatment, however, his condition worsened. Despite the constant pain, weakness, and rapid weight loss, he forced himself to come to the office. He struggled to complete his work, feeling like he couldn't let Huldah down. She needed him, he maintained. But finally he couldn't press on any longer. Something had to be done.

Carol took him to the hospital. After a brief examination, the doctor shook his head in defeat. "You've brought in a dead man. There is nothing we can do. The cancer has spread."

Huldah remained in constant contact with B.W.'s wife and associates, seeking information on his condition.

The congregation in Calcutta fasted and prayed for B.W.'s healing.

One night while Huldah was praying, she felt an assurance that God was going to heal her friend and coworker. "God, surely You won't take B.W. too. I need him," she prayed. "How can we accomplish all this without him?"

Huldah was in her office when she received a phone call. B.W. had passed away. Her body went cold. She couldn't work. She put her head on her desk and cried.

She went home and sat on the corner of her bed, allowing the tears to flow. Once again she picked up her *Living Bible* and in a tense tone said, "God, what in the world are You doing to me? First Mark, then B.W. Who do You expect to help me? God, if I ever needed You, I need You right now. Please help me." She opened her Bible to Daniel 10:17-19 and knew God was speaking comfort to her: "For my strength is gone and I can hardly breathe. Then the one who seemed to be a man touched me again, and I felt my strength returning. 'God loves you very much,' he said; 'don't be afraid! Calm yourself; be strong—yes, strong!' Suddenly, as he spoke those words, I felt stronger and said to him, 'Now you can go ahead . . . for you have strengthened me."

Instantly Huldah was energized with faith, knowing she did not need to fret any longer. She was reminded that her assurance didn't come from within; it was a gift from Almighty God.

A New Beginning

For 11 years B.W. had served as executive director. At a memorial service in Calcutta, Huldah said, "He was a close friend and a valuable associate in the ministry in Calcutta, which he demonstrated by his genuine love for the people in our city and being sensitive to their needs."

She broke her sentence for a moment to fend off tears. Then she continued.

"He traveled with Pastor extensively in meetings, and since Pastor's passing he has assisted so much in fund-raising for various projects, especially our new church. He will be greatly missed by us all, as we recall the annual visits he made and the warmth of his friendship and love for every department of our work and for each one. Our loss is certainly heaven's gain and because he is in heaven it brings heaven that much closer to us."

God did not desert Huldah or the Mission. Just prior to B.W.'s death, the board of directors of Mission of Mercy had merged the ministry with the Bethesda Foundation—an organization committed to funding missions projects around the world. Bethesda had enthusiastically supported many of Mark and Huldah's visions through the years. And now God had brought in fine Christians like David Burdine, Don Beard, Dan Vagle, and others to stand with Huldah—to ensure that the miracles of Mission of Mercy continued. And continue they did.

CHAPTER SEVEN

He Left His Mark

"Huldah," a close friend commented, "Mark truly is living on in the lives of the young men he touched and trained. Look around you."

Huldah knew that statement was true. Five pastors of the English-speaking congregation came through the church's youth camps and schools. Some came from poverty-stricken families. Like employees in every department, these pastors could share testimonies of how Mark, Huldah, and the Mission had made a difference in their lives.

One pastor came from a nominal Christian home. He had never heard of the Mission or the Buntains until one day friends invited him to attend the church's youth camp.

"I'd like to go, but I don't have any rupees to pay the camp fees," the young man responded.

"We will talk to Pastor and Auntie Buntain; they will want you to come," he was told.

As expected, Auntie Buntain offered to pay the fees. At that camp meeting, the young man went to the altar and accepted Jesus Christ as his personal Savior.

Upon returning home he told his parents of his decision. They gave him two options: "You are either our son or leave this house and follow this new religion. Make up your mind."

He prayed to his newfound God until he had a peace about leaving home.

He spent some nights in parks, sleeping on patches of grass and pavement. Many days he went without food, bathing only when friends invited him to their home. He padded the holes in his shoes with cardboard, and he often spent nights shivering under doorways to shield himself from the rains.

Living alone, without shelter and a supply of food, made home much more appealing. He longed for the day he could return to his family, but the price they demanded was too great. He wasn't willing to surrender his faith in Jesus Christ.

His parents thought he would eventually return to the nest and agree to their terms. They were surprised, however, by his prolonged commitment to his faith.

Eventually *they* surrendered and invited him to return home on new terms. They would permit him to stay in their home as long as he obeyed one rule: Each evening he had to be home by 7:00. The young man agreed. Thus, he attended the first 20 minutes of the church services, then raced home to keep his pledge to his parents.

His faith mounted. Before long he was one of the leaders of the church youth group. He was a motivating force behind the young people distributing tracts on Saturday mornings. He was an evangelist in the truest sense. A day wouldn't pass that he didn't tell someone about Jesus.

As a last resort his parents decided to send him away to school to earn a teacher's certificate. Though poor, the parents were desperate to give their son a chance at financial stability and status. Furthermore, they wanted him to shed his newfound religion. "When he leaves the city he will forget Jesus," his parents said.

Shortly before the young man was to take his college entrance exams, he injured his knee in a tragic bike accident. His friend was killed.

The injury required weeks of recuperation. While in bed recovering, he sensed God encouraging him to go into pastoral ministry instead of teaching. So when he was on his feet again, he paid a visit to Pastor Mark.

"Do you believe God has called you?" Mark asked.

"Yes," he said. "And I believe I should go to Bible college rather than become a teacher."

"Then why don't you go? I'm behind you," Mark said, unaware that the young man's parents did not approve.

"My parents want me to become a teacher instead," he said. "They feel very strongly about this. What should I do?"

Mark hesitated. "I see. I can't tell you what to do, but I will pray for your parents and that God will speak to them."

A few days later, the young man returned to Mark's office carrying his completed application for Bible college. "Pastor, I have another problem. I do not have money to pay the tuition fees," he said nervously. "Can I apply for some financial assistance?"

Mark scribbled his signature on the young man's application. "It has already been taken care of. Mrs. Buntain and I believe God will supply your need."

The young man's eyes filled with tears. He sprang from his chair and hugged Pastor Buntain.

His family was not pleased by his decision. The young man responded to their disapproval, saying, "God has called me to be a pastor. That's all I know and that's what I'm going to do. I love you, but nothing or no one is going to change my mind. I hope you'll understand."

Upon arriving at Bible college, the young man received word that Pastor Buntain had passed away. He cried for hours, confused why God would take his mentor from him—a man who was touching so many lives.

He also feared his scholarship would be lost and he would have to return home. He was relieved when, some days later, Huldah assured him the scholarship would be honored.

"Just make me proud. Make Uncle Mark proud by studying hard," she said.

"Yes, Auntie," he replied. "I will make you proud, and someday I hope I can return to help you in the church and Mission. I want to repay you for all you have done for me."

Months passed. And while the young man was in college, his parents didn't respond to his letters. When he decided to enroll in Bible college and spurn their offer to send him to teacher's training school, it was as if he had divorced himself from the family.

After graduating from Bible college, the young man accepted an invitation to join the church's pastoral staff and work with Huldah. He worked hard to show his gratitude to Mrs. Buntain. She had been used by God to give him a new life, and he wanted nothing more than to say thank you through his faithful service.

One Sunday morning he stepped to the pulpit to lead the congregation in prayer. There, sitting in the back row, were his parents. He wanted to shout, run to their pew, and embrace them. But he restrained himself and uttered the most fervent prayer of his life.

That morning his parents learned about Jesus—the One who had changed the life of their son. Following the service, they begged their son to come home. The young pastor surged with confidence, knowing his family's salvation was only a matter of time.

Today they are serving God and attending church faithfully. And, needless to say, they are proud of their son.

Running From God

Many years ago, as a young missionary, Mark and a doctor routinely scaled five flights of stairs to treat a child stricken with tuberculosis. One night the boy began hemorrhaging, and Mark rushed over to pray that God would spare the lad's life. The hemorrhaging instantly stopped. That night the boy's health began to improve. The symptoms disappeared.

Years later, on the verge of manhood, the boy's elder brother took him to England. But there he fell away from God. Parties and alcohol consumed his life. Yet, after each indulgence, he was laden with guilt and dissatisfaction. His search for happiness and purpose had gone nowhere. He began to search his soul, to ponder his spiritual heritage and the Bible verses he had learned as a child in Calcutta. He thought about the investment Pastor and Mrs. Buntain had made in his life. He thought about his healing. Having fallen to many of Satan's enticements, he yearned for a new beginning. One night, while alone in his London apartment, he rededicated his life to Jesus.

In time, largely because of David Wilkerson's book, *The Cross and the Switchblade,* God began dealing with him about working with young people. Specifically, he felt a desire to return to Calcutta after being away for many years. To himself he said, *That's so unlikely. How is it possible?*

One evening he attended a church service in England and entered the prayer line. The guest speaker knew nothing about the young man's background. Yet, when he touched the young man's forehead, he prophesied, "You are going back to Calcutta. You will minister with young people and work with newborn babes in Christ."

Following the service, the recommitted Christian ran home and fell on his knees: "God, thank You for speaking. I will serve You for the rest of my life. Just help me get back to Calcutta."

The young man traced Mark to a hotel in the States, and he placed a phone call.

Mark answered, "What can I do for you, buddy? It's been a long time since I've heard from you."

"Pastor, God is dealing with me about coming back to Calcutta and working with young people."

"When can you come?" Mark posed, seemingly not surprised by the phone call.

Little did the young man know that a pastor who had been serving with Mark and Huldah was having to leave Calcutta. The Buntains had been praying that God would send a replacement who could minister to troubled teenagers.

Mark repeated his question: "Well, when can you come?"

"Pastor, I'll be there in January," he answered.

In the years since, this man has stood faithfully by the Buntains. He has contributed by overseeing the boys' home and Teen Challenge program.

Son of a Wealthy Man

A wealthy non-Christian family enrolled their young son in the Mission's school. They had the financial means to send him to any private school in Calcutta; the Mission's school was selected because of its scholastic standing and reputation for developing good discipline.

The teenager could not help being influenced by the kindness of the Buntains. As a boy he was once scampering through the compound when Mark's large frame stepped in front of him like a roadblock. "Wait, son, you shouldn't be running with a pencil in your hand. You could fall and poke out your eye."

The boy smiled. "Yes, sir."

From that day the boy observed how Mark cared for children, providing food, medical care, and education. Through the years, he often wondered what motivated this man to care so deeply for so many children.

One summer he attended youth camp. During a morning chapel service, the tug on his heart to accept Jesus as his Savior was becoming unbearable. The preacher asked those who were wanting to be delivered from drugs, alcohol, or cigarettes to walk to the front of the room. That didn't apply to him, but he felt the pull to go forward anyway.

He had to do something. He couldn't wait any longer. Abruptly, he ran out of the meeting. Outside, on the football field, he fell on his knees and gave his heart to Jesus Christ.

His parents were shocked to discover the boy had become a Christian. They thought he had been brainwashed.

To hear Pastor Mark preach, the young man would leave the house pretending he was going to play basketball. Instead, he would run to a friend's house, gather his clothes and Bible, then proceed to the church.

His charade began to unravel when his parents discovered a Bible hidden in his cupboard, which they promptly confiscated. He decided not to put up a fight. He kept his faith to himself. Every night, in his bed, he prayed under his sheets. Many nights were spent dreaming he would one day be a preacher like Mark.

When he was 21 he decided it was time to be baptized in water. He also decided to attend Bible college.

While the young man was away at Bible college, his father's health deteriorated. The disorder was diagnosed as a growth below the liver, so the "wayward" son returned home to express his love and respect for his distant father.

Huldah and the congregation held an all-night prayer meeting on behalf of this man whom none of them had ever met. Many sent him get-well cards and paid him visits in the hospital.

The show of concern for his health left the father speechless. Many had said that God would heal him. But the stoic father dismissed the prophecies as "Christian nonsense."

The father was perhaps the most surprised when the physician, wearing a bewildered smile, remarked, "Sir, there is no growth here anymore. You are well and free to go home. It has disappeared."

The father's face was a potpourri of emotions: relief, confusion, and curiosity.

Commenting later to his son, the father said, "Please tell all your friends at the church that I am grateful." That was the beginning of his parents' change of heart. They did not accept Jesus immediately, nor did they understand it fully. But they knew there was something extraordinary about their son's newfound religion.

After completing his college education, the young man accepted a pastoral position at the Assemblies of God church.

The Flood

In a city far from Calcutta, a young man was raised in the home of a non-Christian businessman. He enrolled in the finest university in his region. It was here that a professor told him about Jesus—the Son of God. He rejected what he heard without consideration.

Shortly thereafter, he fell sick with fever and was confined to his bed. He was so ill that when floods were predicted and other students evacuated the hostel, he didn't have the strength to move. A classmate left to get transportation. But before he returned, water engulfed the college hostel and the sickly young man was swept into the raging waters.

Fearing he was about to drown, the young man cried out, "If there is a God—the One my professor told me about—please save me."

In a matter of minutes, he was pulled out of the water by fishermen who saw him struggling to stay afloat.

A few days later, he read a sign announcing church services. He found the church and told the pastor of his experience. That day he surrendered his life fully to Jesus Christ.

He shared the story with his family. Despite their objections, he felt God wanted him to go to the Mission's Bible college in Calcutta.

Some time later, he joined Mrs. Buntain's pastoral staff, where he has been used to help many people in need.

An Orphan

Huldah appeared at the front door of the home of a 15-year-old boy. His father had just been diagnosed with terminal cancer. Since his mother had died of tuberculosis three years earlier, he was now the man of the house. He was having to care for his younger brother and two sisters. That day Huldah placed the girls in homes where they could receive adequate care. She then took the two brothers to the boys' home.

The father's health failed quickly. On his death bed, he told his eldest son, "If I die, trust God . . . but stay with the Buntains. Make them proud of you. God and the Buntains will have to care for you now. Remember, I love you, and we'll be together again someday in heaven."

The boy never forgot his father's parting words. He depended on the Buntains, and they took good care of him. Whenever possible, Mark and Huldah visited him and his brother at the boys' home, encouraging and loving them.

"We love you," Mark reminded them on each visit.

With tooth-filled smiles, the two brothers responded, "We love you too, Pastor."

As the years passed, the older boy made the Buntains proud. He cared for the younger kids and continued to do well in his studies. After completing college, he could have left the home and pursued his own affairs, but he knew the boys needed him; the

Buntains needed him. So he stayed and worked in the boys' home. He continued counseling the boys and praying with them at night before he tucked them into their beds. He helped them with their homework and studies. In his eyes, every boy was his younger brother. He cared for them as he knew Pastor and Mrs. Buntain would.

As a reward for his faithfulness, the missionaries helped him attend Bible college. Upon graduation, he returned to serve on the pastoral staff with Huldah.

Today he can be seen leading a worship service, preaching, and praying for the sick. But his greatest pastoral privilege is to visit the boys' home. At least once a week he can be found leading them in prayer and teaching Bible studies. To the boys, he is one helping to fill Pastor Buntain's shoes.

Raised in the Mission

Many years ago, a man from Shanghai traveled the seven seas on a British merchant ship. When the war broke out, a Japanese destroyer sank his vessel. He survived the attack and eventually landed in Calcutta. With what money he had saved, he started a small Chinese restaurant in the heart of the city. The business flourished. The owner and his Christian wife enjoyed a prosperous life until the British left Calcutta. Because most Indians shunned the restaurant's specialty of beef and pork, the man had to close his shop and take a job as a chef at another restaurant. Shortly thereafter, his wife died of pneumonia. The grief-stricken chef had no choice but to enroll his little son in the Mission's school, while he worked 16-hour days.

The child grew up attending the school, Sunday school, and youth group. His dimpled cheeks, enthusiasm, and cute giggle endeared him to Mark and Huldah. At a young age he would recite Bible verses at church and school programs without a shred of fear. He spoke loudly and clearly. Huldah often remarked, "He'll surely be a preacher some day."

As a teenager, the boy became president of the church's youth group. It didn't surprise anyone that he sounded like his mentor when he preached to the young people. He had heard Mark preach so many times from the front row of the sanctuary.

After attending Bible college, he returned to the Mission to assume a key pastoral position. He helped lead the expansion of West Bengal Bible College and assisted Huldah in pastoring the church. But his career nearly came to a tragic conclusion one afternoon when the car he was driving caught fire. Within seconds smoke consumed his vehicle. Pedestrians threw water and mud to dowse the flames. The young pastor escaped, but he had to be hospitalized for inhaling toxic gases.

Huldah entered the pastor's hospital room. He was sitting up, drinking a bottle of water.

"How are you feeling?" she asked in a motherly way.

"I'm feeling better, thank God. Did you hear what happened?"

"Yes. Thank the Lord you got out of the car when you did. The enemy is trying every way he can to interfere with our work, isn't he?"

"It's spiritual warfare," the pastor declared. "The enemy doesn't want us to continue spreading the name of Jesus."

"That's right," Huldah said. "Let me pray for you."

The pastor bowed his head. Huldah took his hand. Instantly she flashed back to when he was a boy, and how she spent long hours with him and often led him by the hand across the compound.

Leaving the hospital, she saw two young doctors standing nearby and remembered how they were brought to the Mission school and later sent by Mark to medical school. She glanced at a number of nurses who had been blessed by the school of nursing. One of the nurses was the sister of one of the church pastors. Huldah couldn't help but reflect on the faithfulness of God. *Thank You, Father, for giving me such fine people to work with,* Huldah prayed silently. *Thank You for their faithfulness. Please touch their lives and make them instruments for reaching this city with Your gospel. How grateful I am for the young people You have been preparing for many years to serve this church and Mission. They have been trained for such a time as this.*

En route to her office, Huldah paused at Mark's grave. She stood there for a few minutes with her head bowed. With tears in her eyes, she said, "Surely, Mark, you are living on in the lives you touched and trained. They will carry on your mission."

CHAPTER EIGHT

Living Miracles

"I regret having to disturb you so late, Mrs. Buntain," exclaimed the stately guard at the entrance of her apartment.

"It's quite all right," she said, her door slightly ajar. "What is it?"

"There is a lady downstairs. She is crying and saying that her son is dying. She is begging to see you."

Without a word, Huldah descended the stairway to where the visitor was waiting in the darkness.

"What is the problem?" Huldah asked.

Exasperated, the woman said, "My son is seriously ill. He is dying."

"What is the cause?"

"He has a kidney problem. We have come very far to see you. We heard about you; we heard you will help people like us."

Huldah suddenly realized the sacrifice this mother had made to arrive at her front door.

The woman's face was filled with fear. She told Huldah she had tried to find help everywhere, but to no avail.

"Where's the boy?" Huldah asked.

"He is lying in the emergency room in your hospital."

Huldah thought for a moment, and then taking a pen and paper, she wrote a note to the doctor instructing him to admit the teenager and give him medical attention.

Handing the note to the visitor, Huldah said, "Take this message to the hospital. I'll visit your son tomorrow morning."

The woman, with tears filling her eyes, clasped Huldah's hands with extreme gratitude.

Huldah visited the sick boy as promised. His condition was serious, his body terribly thin. Huldah patted his hand. "We will pray that God will help you."

The boy was too weak to respond.

Day after day, Huldah and other pastors prayed with the parents and their sickly child. Yet the boy's condition worsened. He was an awful sight. Tubes and monitor wires were running to his body. His complexion was pale. His eyes were deep-set and lifeless. He was gasping for every breath.

Huldah asked one of the pastors to go pray for the child. An hour later, the young pastor returned, saying, "I've seen many sick people. I've seen people die, but that is the most horrible case I've ever seen. Mrs. Buntain, barring a miracle, the doctors think he may not make it. His kidneys are failing."

Within minutes, Huldah was at the hospital. She shook off the morbid thought of death and laid her hand on the boy's head, praying, "In Jesus' name, I ask that You heal this boy as a testimony of Your glory."

She felt no warmth pass through her hands or heat radiating from the boy's body. His face registered nothing. His limbs didn't move. She prayed again. Nothing. That afternoon she left knowing doctors were predicting he would be gone by morning.

Before the sun cast its rays over the city the following morning, Huldah entered the hospital. She was met by a white-coated, gray-haired doctor in the hallway.

"How is he?" Huldah asked stonily.

"He seems to be improving slightly," the doctor said hesitantly.

"Praise God," she declared.

"But, Mrs. Buntain, he still needs a kidney transplant," the doctor added with a look of concern. "It will require the work of a specialist at a larger hospital."

Undaunted, Huldah sensed God stirring her to action. The transplant would cost about $20,000, but saving the boy's life was worth every penny. She instructed the doctors to make arrangements for the operation, though uncertain where she would find the money.

The boy's father was willing to donate a kidney, but there was a question whether the organ would be acceptable due to the man's long bout with alcoholism. He had been instantly delivered of alcohol during a church service, but all feared there was no reversing its lingering effect. Doctors ran tests and were astounded to find that the kidney was a perfect match and in good condition.

Bewildered surgeons told Huldah that when they removed the father's kidney they found it was like that of a child. "It was as though this man had never taken a sip of alcohol in his life," a doctor said.

Within days, both the boy and his father were sitting up in their hospital beds conversing with nurses and fellow patients.

Naturally Huldah rejoiced over the outcome, but it didn't take long for her to experience the bittersweet taste of reality. God had surely performed one miracle, and she prayed He would perform another. A $20,000 medical bill remained.

Marilyn Hickey, copastor of a church in Colorado, came to Calcutta to preach a series of messages.

During one of the services she asked people to come forward who needed a miracle. As she approached the mother of this boy—who was set to undergo the transplant—Marilyn said, "Your son will not die; he will be raised up for the glory of God." Marilyn knew nothing about the woman and her son. The Holy Spirit had revealed this to her. Later, Huldah and the mother related the story to Marilyn, who took a special interest in the case.

Before Marilyn left the city, she again heard the voice of God and said, "Our church will help pay the bill. I feel that is what God would have us do."

Filled with gratitude for Marilyn's generosity, Huldah prayed silently, *God, You saved this boy's life. You saved his family. And now You have sent this beautiful woman to relieve this financial burden from me. I will be forever grateful.*

Today the young boy and his entire family attend church regularly.

A Healed Heart

One of Huldah's parishioners had endured a heart problem for 10 years. There were days the woman found breathing laborious and she lacked the energy to walk the short distance to church. Much of the time she was confined to a mat on the floor of her hovel.

When her family thought the end was near, they admitted her to the hospital.

Doctors advised Huldah that heart surgery was necessary to save the woman. "We will do our best, but she still may not make it," a physician warned. "This is a severe case. We can't guarantee she will come through the operation alive, but we have to proceed. We don't have any time to waste. This woman is living on borrowed time."

Once again Huldah held a life in her hands. The intricate surgery would require the work of a highly paid heart specialist from a neighboring hospital. Neither the woman, nor her family, had the resources to pay for an operation that would cost more than they would earn in a lifetime. They were preoccupied with earning enough money to eat each day. So it was left to Huldah to decide if the surgery was affordable.

"We will find some way to raise the money for the operation," Huldah vowed to the woman's husband. "Please get her into surgery as soon as possible."

Huldah and two other pastors gathered around the woman's hospital bed prior to the open-heart surgery.

"Mrs. Buntain, I'm scared," she said, her lips trembling. Her eyes were glazed as one who knew death was imminent.

"God can give you peace," Huldah answered. "Let's pray that He will do that."

The woman squeezed Huldah's hand like one hanging onto life.

"Father," Huldah prayed, "this dear friend has suffered many months with this condition. Give her peace right now. Guide the surgeon's hands. We pray she will have a speedy recovery and will be restored to perfect health."

At the time Huldah didn't know that doctors had given the patient only a 20 percent chance to live.

The day following the surgery Huldah reentered the woman's room. Huldah hadn't heard the doctors' prognosis, so she didn't know what to expect. Would the woman be clinging to life? Would she be conscious? Would she ever speak again? What Huldah saw nearly caused her to grab for her own heart. The woman was sitting on the side of her bed smiling, combing her hair. Her surgery had left a scar from her navel to the base of her neck, yet she looked like she could have marched out of the hospital without a helping hand.

"God has given you a miracle," Huldah said.

With a single tear sliding down her cheek, she said, "Yes, He has. May I come to church on Sunday? I want to thank my friends for praying for me. I want to show them what God can do."

Huldah's first inclination was to advise against her request, but she bit her tongue. "Let's ask the doctor," Huldah said. "If he says it's okay . . ."

The visiting physician was amazed at his patient's rapid recovery, suggesting that the mystic powers had smiled upon her. "Go home and thank the gods for having mercy on you," he said.

"There is just one God who helped me," the woman answered with a smile. "He healed my heart, and I will serve Him the rest of my life."

The doctor nodded, for he wasn't about to dispute her claims.

The following Sunday the woman was transported to the church so she could testify of God's power in the service. The congregation had prayed diligently for their beloved friend; so when they saw her walk onto the platform, they erupted into praise for answered prayer. Many knew that without a healing miracle her splendid smile would have never again graced their sanctuary. Seeing her behind the pulpit was another testimony to the power of prayer.

Today the woman can be seen carrying bags of rice, walking stairs, and working like a teenager. She is one of the most faithful members of the congregation, grateful she can walk between her hovel and the church without pain.

The Paralyzed Walk

The little girl was her mother's prized possession. Her copper skin, dimples, pigtails, and pure white teeth gave her a natural beauty that made her stand out from the crowd. She was talented, often taking the leading role in many of the church and school programs.

One Sunday morning she awoke with a high fever and could not attend church. By late afternoon her neck had become stiff and her temperature was rising. Her frantic parents rushed her to the hospital. By the time they arrived she was paralyzed, her toes strangely turned up. Her eyes were fixed, her eyesight blurred.

During the Sunday night service, just as Huldah was standing to lead in prayer, the mother ran into the sanctuary. She raced to the platform and handed Huldah a note that told of the daughter's condition.

The congregation immediately went to prayer. Huldah rushed to the hospital and found the room filled with doctors, relatives, and close friends.

"Mrs. Buntain," the mother said, "they are now preparing her for a lumbar puncture. They do not know what is wrong. Some feel it is meningitis, while other specialists feel it is something else."

Huldah took the mother by the hand and quietly stepped to the bed where the girl's body was resting. The child's eyes were wide open with fear.

Huldah asked the girl, "Do you believe Jesus can heal you?"

She rolled her eyes toward Huldah. She mustered all the strength she could to say, "Auntie, yes."

"Do you remember a few years ago when you were ill with jaundice and the Lord touched you?"

The girl's eyes responded yes.

Huldah said a simple prayer, concluding with "Amen."

On cue, the child screamed, "I can move my head. I can move my feet."

She began to turn her head from one side to another.

The doctors who had been talking quietly on the other side of the room ran to the bed when they saw the child moving.

"What did you do to the child?" a doctor asked.

"I prayed for her," Huldah replied.

The mother and father began telling the specialists about Jesus Christ and divine healing.

The doctors were in silent awe.

Within a short time, the child was sitting up in bed and asking for something to eat.

The following day, nurses had a difficult time keeping the girl in her bed. She wanted to go room-to-room telling patients that Jesus had healed her.

Because of the healing, friends of the girl's family began attending the church. Sitting in the balcony one Sunday morning, a businessman and his family committed their lives to God. The following week, the family was in an automobile accident and the man was killed. The wife and children were spared injury.

At the funeral, Huldah related the story of how this man had found Jesus Christ just days before his death.

"God will go to great lengths to save a lost soul," she said. "He loves us so much."

The widow nodded her head, for she was grateful to know her husband was now in the presence of Jesus.

Blood Poisoning

Blood poisoning had forced a boy into a coma. A city physician said there was nothing more that could be done to save him. With no hope and the forecast bleak, the vice-principal of the boy's school brought the prayer request to the Sunday night church service. In the middle of the service, one of the pastors felt impressed to pray for the child and invited the congregation to join him. "You're the God of the impossible," the pastor prayed. "We have seen You perform one miracle after another. Now we pray in the name of Jesus Christ that this boy—right now in his room—will be set free and healed, and the doctors will be baffled."

At the very moment the congregation prayed, the boy bolted from his coma. His eyes opened. He moved his lips to speak, but nothing came out. He tried again, and this time he was able to call out to his mother.

Excitedly, the parents summoned the physician. The doctors subsequently warned that his awakening was a sign that death was imminent.

But when the boy's blood test was completed, city doctors were indeed baffled. The report showed no infection, no poison. The boy was healed, and news spread throughout the community that the "miracle church" had prayed him back to life.

A Traffic Accident

A Buddhist man, his wife, and their young son were traveling to a dinner engagement. Heavy monsoon rains had flooded the dark streets. A truck collided with their car, and the impact threw their son into the dashboard. Immediately he writhed in pain, clutching his stomach. "Daddy, help me. Mommy, help me!" he cried.

Fortunately the accident occurred near the Mission hospital. A short time later, the boy was wheeled into the operating room. While they waited for the surgery to be completed, the young parents noticed a small sign near the elevator. It read: "Call unto Me, and I will answer you, and show you great and mighty things." The mother uttered, "Jesus, please help us."

They had sent their son to the Mission school but, as Buddhists, they had never prayed to Jesus before.

When Huldah learned of the tragedy, she urged the congregation to pray. "The operation is in the hospital, but the spiritual battle is in the church," she said.

Huldah was not surprised the surgery was a success. She knew God had answered their prayers. But she was disappointed that the father had not turned to God following his son's recovery. Instead, he openly refused to believe in the healing power of God.

A few months later, the child returned to the hospital. Doctors discovered the intestine had become entwined. The boy was rolling in pain.

Meanwhile, the father stared skeptically at his wife who was using every spare moment to pray. "Why us?" he cried.

Through the prayers of the church and the personal visits of Huldah, the mother received a word of prophecy: "There will be a healing in your home for the glory of God."

The boy was discharged, but he soon returned a third time. While his tormented son screamed in agony, the Buddhist man finally acknowledged his need for God. He made his way to the church and sat through one of the services. Huldah felt that if he would simply come forward during the altar call God would intervene for his dying child.

At the end of the service, the young father went forward. Huldah prayed for his salvation and the child's health.

When Huldah revisited the boy's hospital room a few hours later, the father could be heard in a loud voice announcing his salvation and declaring that his boy had been healed. The pain in the boy's stomach had ceased, never to return.

Today they are ardent Christians and active in many of the church's ministries.

Murdered Mother

A young woman hiked out of the jungles of India, over rugged mountains, and across countless streams to get to the Mission's West Bengal Bible College. Her feet were swollen from the epic journey. Though the Bible college had already reached full capacity, officials couldn't bring themselves to turn her away. She had paid too great a price to study God's Word.

In the following years, she studied hard to become one of the college's star pupils. She was the first student in the library in the morning and the last to leave at night. Other students admired her strong faith and determination to serve God.

One day she was found crying outside the library. She had just received a letter informing her that her mother was dead. Students gathered around their friend and prayed. They held her in their arms and cried with her.

When her tears stopped, she was asked, "Do you want to leave and go back for the funeral?"

"No. That's impossible. It takes many weeks for letters to arrive from my home. The funeral is already over. Besides, if I go now I'll miss my final exams. My mother wouldn't want me to do that. I'll take my tests, then go."

Two weeks passed. She entered the principal's office with tears glistening on her cheeks. She had just learned more details of her mother's death. "I know how she died and who the murderers are," she said in a surprisingly passive tone.

"Have you notified the police?" the principal asked, his voice laced with outrage.

She paused. "No, I believe Jesus wants me to pray for them."

"Well, who did this?"

"My mother was an evangelist. She would go through the villages preaching the gospel. In one village some men threatened her. They said they were going to kill her the next time she tried to preach to their people. She didn't let them scare her. She went back, and they're the ones who did it."

"Are you sure?" he asked, noting the lack of vengeance in her words.

"Yes. There is no doubt," she replied, nodding absently. Her dark eyes stared without expression as if seeing the village in her mind.

"Is there anything we can do?" he asked.

She shook her head. "No, it's in God's hands now."

The student, some weeks later, walked through the graduation line. She walked to the microphone to be interviewed by the college principal. "What's next for you?" he asked. "What will you do with your life?"

With tears of joy, she said, "I'm going to take my mother's place. I'm going back to my village and share Jesus as an evangelist."

Huldah and the principal prayed with her that God would guide her future and ministry.

Following graduation, the young woman left Calcutta. Everyone continues to pray for her, hopeful she is alive and winning more villagers to Jesus Christ.

A Drowning Victim?

A young boy shed his clothing and jumped into the lake. After a few minutes, his arms went limp with exhaustion. He submerged and never resurfaced. Two friends retrieved his body from the water and dragged him to the shore. There were no signs of life. No heartbeat. No breathing.

His Christian mother cried, "Oh God, how could You let this happen to me? Why has this happened to my son?"

Her mouth tightened as the fear mounted.

Villagers began to sympathize with her, but, at the same time, they criticized her faith in God. "Only a witch doctor can help you now," they said.

She didn't listen to their persuasion. She sent for the pastor of one of the Mission's outreach churches. When the pastor arrived, a mob was still crowded around the boy's lifeless body. They had already given him up for dead.

"What can *he* do?" a villager shouted toward the pastor. "He is powerless. Call the witch doctor."

"I'm as human as you are," the pastor replied. "I can't do anything, but I know Someone who can."

"Who?" the villagers asked. "Is *he* a witch doctor?"

"No, His name is Jesus. Why don't we ask Him to touch this boy?"

Villagers didn't know the Bible or how to pray, but in unison they began to repeat the name of Jesus.

The "dead" child suddenly let out a loud sneeze; water gushed from his nostrils and mouth.

Villagers stepped back in amazement.

The mother shouted for joy.

The lad sat up, his mouth opening with a startled look on his face. He then vomited more water. His eyes flicked from side-to-side as if asking, *Why are so many people staring at me?* When the boy was hoisted to his feet, villagers stepped back with astonishment.

Then, with the hysteria of a child who had lost his parents in a shopping mall, he broke through the circle and ran back to the village.

Villagers who once jeered the pastor were now wanting to touch this "holy" man. They wanted to ask him questions about Jesus. They wanted to learn how they could know Him, too.

"What God can do this? We will serve Him if you tell us His name," they said.

The pastor told them the story of Jesus' death and resurrection, then led many of them in the sinner's prayer.

Swimming With Sharks

Four young men carried out their daily routine. Loading their small boats with a fishing net, they set out on the Bay of Bengal. They positioned their boats so each could hold a corner of the large net. Then the boats collected the catch by moving toward one another and rowing back to shore. This particular day the catch proved to be bountiful. One of the men pointed gleefully to two large sharks inside the net. Sharks yielded high profits due to their medicinal value.

The revelry was broken when one of the boats experienced a sudden jerk, tossing a young fisherman headlong into the net holding the two sharks. His friends were paralyzed with fear, thinking death was imminent. There was no way to rescue him without sacrificing their own lives. The knifing sharks immediately spotted the human flesh.

The young man, a Christian who attended one of the Mission's churches, cried out, "Jesus, Jesus!" He was bobbing frantically in the water. When he surfaced again, he was staring into the fangs of a large shark. He swam toward one of the boats. The sharks gave chase, brushing against his legs before darting away.

His friends pulled him into the boat. The shivering young man turned and stared at the sharks, proclaiming, "Did you see it? It was Jesus who shut the sharks' mouths. Jesus saved my life. He shut the mouths of lions for Daniel in the Bible; He shut the mouths of sharks for me."

His friends were stunned speechless.

"Jesus is alive," he shouted. "Do you hear me? I am alive because He saved me."

News of the miracle spread throughout the region, from village to village. To this day the young fisherman is revered among his people as the one whose God helped him "swim with the sharks" and live to tell about it.

Seeing Jesus

Two boys were raised by parents who denied the existence of Jesus Christ. Their parents permitted them to attend the Mission's Christian school only because they thought the education was superior and would one day provide greater opportunity in the marketplace.

The eldest son was curious about this One known as Jesus, though unwilling to investigate a religion that contradicted his parents' beliefs. Time and again he heard his teachers and classmates talk about Jesus. Still, he hadn't yet seen or heard anything to convince him Jesus wasn't what his parents claimed He was: a mythical figure from the West. "Until I see Him I won't believe in Him," the teenager vowed.

One afternoon, alone in his bedroom, he felt Someone touch his back. He turned and saw an image of One he knew was Jesus. Then, just as quickly, the image disappeared.

The boy began to weep uncontrollably. "Jesus, I accept that You are real," he prayed. "You have shown yourself to me. Now I will serve You."

From that day forward the boy's life was changed. He became involved in the church's youth group and began telling all his friends about the encounter with his Savior.

Sometime later, the younger brother asked, "Is it true that you saw Jesus?"

"Yes, it is true."

"Why are you going to church all the time?"

"Because Jesus appeared to me. He touched me," he replied.

The younger son stared into his brother's eyes. He read nothing but sincerity, yet he laughed without mercy. Endlessly he ridiculed his brother, accusing him of losing his mind.

"This is not real," he said acidly. "I don't know what you saw, but it wasn't Jesus."

"It *was* Jesus, and if you ask Him I believe He will reveal Himself to you as well."

"I don't want to see it—whatever it was," he sneered.

Three months later, the younger brother was sitting in the same bedroom. He felt Someone tap his shoulder. He pivoted, expecting to see his brother or mother. Instead, he was alone. He felt ice cold to his fingertips. Immediately he was aware that Jesus had touched him.

He said nervously, "Jesus, I now know You are real, and I want to serve You, too."

The two boys, one afternoon, confessed their respective experiences to their mother. They feared her response, expecting her to laugh or question their sanity in protest. Surprisingly their mother did not abruptly dismiss their claims. Instead she said, "I want to hear more. Invite one of the church's pastors to come to our home."

Today she is a faithful member of the church and can be seen sitting next to her lovely two sons. Their testimony has changed many lives and remains a source of blessing to all.

Death of a Father

A horrified young boy witnessed his drug-addicted father getting hit by a train. The boy tearfully related the incident in graphic detail, slurring syllables as he struggled to maintain his composure. The tragedy often haunted him, vivid nightmares awakening him at all hours. Experts said the child would never fully recover from the trauma. "He will always have emotional problems," they said.

When he first came to the boys' home, he kept to himself. At night he pulled the covers over his head to try burying his dreaded memories. When food was served, he ate alone. When others spoke to him, he cowered without response. When the boys played games, he stood off to the side and watched silently. Some counselors feared the professionals were right: maybe the boy would never recover. Huldah and the other pastors weren't ready to give up on the boy. "God brought him to us. He will help us get through to him," she said.

The hum of the automobile engine was a signal that Auntie Buntain had arrived at the boys' home for a visit. Instantly smiling children engulfed the car. The emotionally troubled boy straggled behind, so Huldah set out to find him. She located him staring out a window into the blank sky.

"How are you?" she asked.

He was silent.

"Are you okay?" she repeated.

He said nothing.

Huldah took his hand and looked into his frightened eyes. "We love you. Do you know that? We wouldn't let anything happen to you."

His eyes met hers, and she knew he understood.

She hugged the boy and handed him a candy bar.

He glanced at her to make sure it was all his.

"Yes, go ahead," she said.

He unwrapped the sweet and took a bite. For the first time since he arrived, a smile broke through.

As the months passed, the boy began to speak and play with the other children. He began to feel at home with his new family and feel secure knowing Jesus as his new Father.

Now when Huldah's automobile enters the gates of the boys' home, she can expect the lovely boy to be the first to greet her. And every Sunday he will not leave the church to return to the boys' home until he holds Auntie Buntain's hand and receives a hug.

The Tumor

When a large tumor was found in a woman's uterus, she begged her family to bring her to Mission of Mercy hospital.

Two pastors visited the woman's room while making their regular rounds. "May we pray for you?" they asked.

"I am Buddhist," she said in broken English.

"Yes, but may we pray for you?" a pastor repeated.

The woman consented.

"Dear Jesus, heal her body so she will know You are real," he prayed.

The frightened woman smiled and thanked the pastors for their concern.

But the pastors did not feel their duty was complete. They asked the church to pray on behalf of this woman. She needed a physical healing and a spiritual encounter with Jesus Christ, they said.

Doctors were able to successfully remove the tumor, but they feared the growth was cancerous. It was likely the disease had spread.

At the woman's request, the pastors returned to her bedside. Hearing the doctors' concerns, she was deeply terrified. Her hand quivering, her eyes filling with tears of uncertainty, she said, "Help me. Please pray to your God for me."

The pastors bowed their heads. The woman didn't know to close her eyes.

"Lord, again we pray that this tumor will not be cancerous," a pastor said. "And when it is not, may this dear woman know You are alive, that You are the one true God."

The woman again had tears in her eyes when the men departed. They could sense that God was moving on her heart.

Outside her room, in the hallway, one of the pastors asked the doctor, "May we call tomorrow to get your report on the tumor?"

The doctor responded, "Honestly, we don't need the report. It *is* cancer. I have no doubt in my mind."

Huldah and the pastors were not willing to surrender hope. They held hands in her office and prayed for another miracle.

The doctor was as surprised as anyone when, the following day, he reported that it *wasn't* cancerous. "God has surely touched this woman," he said. "This had the appearance of cancer."

When the woman heard the news, she beckoned the pastors to the hospital. She asked them if this time *she* could pray.

The pastors glanced knowingly at one another.

"Thank You, Jesus, for helping me," she prayed. "Thank You for dying for my sins. I will serve You the rest of my life."

This woman is now a committed Christian and an active member of Huldah's congregation.

CHAPTER NINE

Village Churches

Beginning in the late 1960s, Mark started to send students from Calcutta to Southern Asia Bible College in Bangalore, South India. His desire was to train nationals so he could one day open his own Bible college in Calcutta. By the 1970s graduates began returning to assist in the church ministries. They began starting outreach programs in village areas ranging from Calcutta to the Bangladesh border in West Bengal. Many workers were trained for areas that needed churches.

Mark saw his dream fulfilled in 1988 when West Bengal Bible College commenced in Calcutta. Since then, God has placed His hand on many young people who are today actively engaged in church ministries.

Kathryn Kuhlman

In the 1960s evangelist Kathryn Kuhlman visited Calcutta. Over tea one afternoon, she asked Mark to share his vision for the city and the neighboring villages.

"I want to see churches built in all of these villages," he said. "I want to see them filled. I want each one to be manned by fine national pastors."

Kathryn broke into a smile. "Do you have a village in need of a church right now?"

"Yes, and we have someone to pastor it," Mark answered. "We just don't have a building for them to meet in."

Kathryn saw the earnestness in Mark's face and said, "I feel the Lord would have me build that church for you."

Before departing Calcutta, she left enough money to build the church.

This was the beginning of a new era—the start of a campaign that would birth many more church buildings in West Bengal. Kathryn's was the seed gift they had been waiting for. For Mark it was as though God was pointing His finger to the outskirts of Calcutta and the suburban areas of the state, saying, *Go!*

Darjeeling

In the 1960s the Buntains had neighbors adjacent to their apartment who were transferred to Darjeeling—

an area tucked between the borders of Bhutan and Nepal. After they had been there a short time, they invited the Buntains to pay them a visit. Mark and Huldah were struck by the beautiful Himalayan Mountains, yet they noticed there were very few churches in Darjeeling.

One morning, before the sun was fully exposed, Mark sat alone on the verandah overlooking the majestic mountains. Huldah could hear him praying. "God, give me these mountains," he said. "Make a way for us to bring them the gospel."

Mark did not live to see his request granted, but God heard his prayer.

A young man, in jail for smuggling drugs, was completely transformed when another inmate led him to Jesus Christ. Upon his release, he contacted missionaries in Nepal for assistance. With their help and guidance he enrolled in Bible college. He quickly grew in his knowledge of the Word of God. Those who observed his rapid spiritual growth knew he was destined to accomplish something great for the Lord. He also displayed a passion for prayer. It was during one of his prayer sessions that God showed him a vision of Darjeeling and the Nepali people who lived in that area.

The people in Nepal thought he would return and help them minister there, but upon graduating, he traveled to Darjeeling without the promise of a building, money, or a congregation. He started the church and had three people in his congregation. His first year was not a success story. In the face of apparent failure, sacrifice, and opposition, he refused to be discouraged or lack faith. He claimed God had sent him there and that He would help him build a church.

The Buntains became acquainted with the young pastor and raised the funds to purchase land for a church. Shortly thereafter, Mark passed away, leaving the young pastor wondering what would become of his building project.

Huldah assured him the project would proceed. About that time, she learned that a parcel adjacent to the land purchased for the Darjeeling church was also available. A hotel was under construction on the property, but an unexpected financial crisis had forced its owner to sell it before completion.

Huldah moved into action. Through the assistance of Mission of Mercy in Canada and director Al McClelland, funds were raised to purchase the property. Plans were then drawn, and the hotel was converted into a three-story church building.

Some months later, Huldah traveled to Darjeeling to attend the dedication service. Huldah wished Mark could have been there to see this magnificent church building and congregation. It was, in part, the fulfillment of his dream.

She also paid a visit to the small hotel that she and Mark had stayed at years earlier. She glanced up at the verandah where Mark had prayed, and thanked God for honoring her husband's prayer. Then she said a prayer of her own: "Lord, may there be many more churches built in these mountains in the years ahead."

Huldah answered the phone one day in her office. She recognized the caller as the pastor from Darjeeling. Excitedly he said, "Sister, there's fire in the hills."

Thinking it was a forest fire, Huldah became concerned. "Oh my, is it anywhere near our churches? I hope none of them will be burned."

The pastor laughed. "Sister—not that kind of fire. Holy Ghost fire."

He went on to explain that the Holy Spirit was moving across the mountains, and revival fires were burning. Churches were springing up all over the hills.

But the burgeoning churches created another worry for Huldah. Some pastors were overseeing a number of village churches, and yet they needed more training. Furthermore, she knew that bringing them to the city and West Bengal Bible College was not the answer.

God gave her the idea for extension Bible schools, where pastors could receive training in the field. The first training center of this kind was launched in Darjeeling. Others have since been started. Pastors and workers come in for studies during the week, then return to their respective churches on weekends. Through this structure many ministers are receiving the training they need to effectively pastor their villages.

Ranchi

One of the last revival campaigns Mark conducted was in Ranchi, a village nearly 200 miles west of Calcutta. While there, he pledged to help the pastor build a large church for the growing congregation.

A faithful missionary had built a very small church there two decades earlier. Now it was inadequate for the needs of the large congregation.

After Mark's death, Huldah assured the pastor in Ranchi that she would do her best to fulfill Mark's pledge—even though she was also raising money for the new sanctuary in Calcutta. Huldah knew Mark was eager to help these people, so she accepted the challenge.

One morning she boarded a train to Ranchi, where she was met by the pastor and his workers. They took her to the site where Mark had preached just prior to his death. They told her thousands had gathered there, and many had surrendered their lives to the Lord. It was the beginning of a great revival, they said. Then they led her to their small church, where they reviewed the drawings for their new building.

Her tour also took her to 37 remote villages. The roads were some of the worst she had ever traveled. She found many Christians living in abject poverty, yet they greeted her at each location with generous smiles. A small service was conducted, with Huldah offering words of encouragement to small congregations, then the tour continued on to another village.

It was about 9:00 in the evening when Huldah arrived back in Ranchi. It had been an arduous 14-hour day, yet Huldah found it difficult to go right to sleep. She was overwhelmed with the potential to advance God's kingdom in so many unreached areas.

Huldah's heart was also touched by the number of committed outreach pastors who were living so sacrificially.

She asked one of the pastors, "How do you support yourself?"

"I am making 100 rupees ($3 U.S.) from my small church," he said, "but it is wonderful how God provides for me each month and meets my needs."

In this farming area, people often brought food to their pastors and gave whatever funds they could to build churches in their villages. They were a portrait of commitment and courage.

The host pastor also took Huldah to a school where many of the students were sponsored by Mission of Mercy. En route, Huldah expressed her desire to launch another extension Bible school to train workers. But, she said, God needs to provide a building.

As she inspected the school complex, she noticed a new building under construction. The building was ideal for an extension Bible school. There was one room large enough for a classroom, a kitchen, and rooms where the pastors could stay.

The pastor shared the story behind the building. A woman had just retired from being a principal at a government school and, in obedience to God, had used her retirement funds to construct the building. She didn't know how the facility was going to be used; she just knew God wanted it built.

Huldah shared with the woman her desire to start an extension Bible school.

The woman replied, "Now I know why God had me construct this building."

Huldah stood in front of the building with tears streaming down her cheeks. She marveled how God had spoken to this woman months earlier in preparation for her visit.

Today, many village churches are under construction and pastors are receiving the training they need at the extension Bible school.

Orissa

Orissa is located south of Calcutta's state, West Bengal, on the east coast of India. The coastal area is on the Bay of Bengal, connecting with the Indian Ocean. Along the coast there are thousands of fishermen and their families who have migrated there from Andhra Pradesh—the state south of Orissa. These impoverished fishermen live in huts built on sand. Their entire livelihood depends on fishing. When the catch is poor, the residents suffer terribly.

When Huldah journeyed to the village of Puri and saw the poor living conditions of fishermen and their families, she was moved. She saw their makeshift huts with grass roofs, and uneducated children wearing tattered clothing. She turned to an accompanying pastor and said, "We must help these people."

The church Mark had helped plant some years earlier was now meeting in a small mud house with no electricity or lights. Huldah stooped to enter the church's front door. The ceiling was low and the quarters small, yet 150 people had gathered for a three-hour service. People were sandwiched together and others outside were trying to listen through windows. The place was like a boiler room. By the time the service ended, Huldah's clothes were soaked with perspiration. Again she whispered, "Somehow we will help them." She left with a heavy burden and determination to help the children get an education.

The following day Huldah walked through the village. Scanning the hundreds of huts and the many children who lived there, she asked the pastor, "Can't we find a building for a school for these children?"

"There is one that I have looked at that I think would be ideal. But we cannot afford it," he said.

Within minutes Huldah and the pastor were walking through the front door of the building that had caught the pastor's eye. Instantly Huldah felt an assurance that this was the place for the school.

Huldah and local pastors met with the landlord and were able to negotiate a lease.

Today in Puri—largely because of the support of Mission of Mercy and child sponsors—hundreds of boys and girls can be seen dressed in beautiful uniforms, sitting in nice classrooms. They have been given full stomachs and a bright future because of God's love and care.

Lionel Maddaford, Huldah's uncle, enjoyed coming to Calcutta each year. One of his favorite spots was Puri. He loved walking along the beach and watching the waves break onto the shore. He often prayed that God would send workers to this area and that churches would be built.

When he died at the age of 91, he left money in his will to build a church. Upon completion it will serve as headquarters for the coastal area churches and much more.

The Mission has expanded its outreaches up and down the coast of Orissa, constructing numerous churches and schools for the families of fishermen.

West of the mountains is another area of Orissa that is also stricken with poverty. Because of drought and famine, many parents were forced to sell their children for a few rupees.

Huldah met a young man who was doing a great work in a number of these poor villages. He wanted to establish more schools and daycare centers, but he did not have the funds to do so. Huldah invited Don Beard, Mission of Mercy president, to join her and some other workers on a trip to see the young man and his work.

The 12-hour journey by train took them to Jhars-guda Village, where there were 400 students Mission of Mercy had already begun helping to support.

The young man shared his vision for a Bible college and more daycare centers and orphanages. He related stories underscoring the need in this area, including one experience on a train: A conductor was walking through the cabin at a train stop, and he noticed what he thought was a bundle of clothing underneath a seat. He reached for the bundle, only to find that it was a three-year-old girl. He took the malnourished child to his office and kept her there until it was obvious her parents had abandoned her. Often female babies are abandoned, sold, or neglected because some in India interpret the birth of a female as a curse from the gods.

Finally, the police were called to take the child. Because they didn't have facilities to care for the girl, the police called the young worker. He and his wife had started orphanages and daycare centers that were so clean and effective, the authorities were willing to entrust them with orphans and abandoned children.

Many children had received hope through these orphanages and daycare centers.

That night, Huldah, Don, and others boarded a train to return to Calcutta. It was the same train on which the little girl was rescued. Huldah and Don conversed as the train chugged along. They discussed what they could do to assist the work in Jharsaguda and how they could participate in giving more children an education and a brighter future. They replayed some of the stories they had heard—namely the child on the train. Huldah and Don had to wipe the tears from their eyes as they pondered the girl's story of triumph. They glanced at each other, their expressions saying, *This is a work deserving of our help. We must try to find more child sponsors to help these boys and girls.*

Graham, Buntain, and Nagaland

Amidst threats and fear of agitation, Billy Graham scheduled a crusade in Nagaland, East India, in an area called "Hills of the Headhunters." Believers there had prayed for years that Graham would visit them. They had heard about him from missionaries in the earliest days of his fame. His crusade in Calcutta in 1956 was also legendary. Finally, in November 1972, he felt led to come to their land. News of his coming spread throughout the region. It was a time to bask in spiritual victory.

But shortly before the meetings, Graham encountered some difficulties that threatened to cancel the crusade. Through much prayer the meetings were held with tremendous results.

Many credited Mark Buntain for his role in preparing hearts for Graham's crusade. Six years earlier,

Mark received an invitation to speak to a large crowd in Nagaland. Like Graham, he also faced an obstacle. This was a restricted area and foreigners needed a permit to travel there. Mark sent back word that, regrettably, it was impossible for him to attend the conference.

He lay awake at night trying to discern God's will. One morning at 4:00, Mark jumped out of bed. "I'm going to Nagaland," he announced.

"Mark," Huldah implored, "you can't go. You don't have a permit. They won't let you on the plane."

"God has told me to go and I'm going," he said.

He packed his bag and set out for the airport. The rest was a miracle: how he was issued a ticket and boarded the plane without anyone asking for a permit; how he was later issued a permit to travel many back roads to the town of Mukokchung, where the conference was being held.

The people prayed all night that Mark would come. At dawn, they heard his jeep approaching up the mountain. They exited their tents to see if indeed God had answered their prayers.

When Mark stepped out of the jeep, he heard a roar of celebration. "Hallelujah!" the people shouted.

There were more than 10,000 in attendance. Some had walked two or three days over mountains to attend the conference.

That night Mark preached for one hour. Afterward, however, they said his message was too short.

A visiting minister confided in Mark prior to the next evening's service. "They don't know about the Holy Spirit," the man said. "So please speak on the Holy Spirit."

Mark preached for three hours, and still the people wanted more. After his sermon he began to pray and speak in tongues. Unbeknownst to Mark, he was actually speaking in a known tongue—the crowd's native language. It was a language familiar to everyone —a mixture of dialects—and Mark was speaking to them about the baptism in the Holy Spirit. They knew they were witnessing a miracle. There was no way Mark could have known their language. That was the birth of many churches in the region—churches that later participated in Graham's crusade.

Today, there are 400 churches, two Bible colleges, 100 schools, International Correspondence Institute offices, and extension Bible schools in the seven states of East India.

In 1994, Huldah received an invitation to speak at a large pastor's conference in Kohima, Nagaland. Surprisingly she was granted a travel permit.

She knew she wasn't Billy Graham or Mark Buntain, so she prayed that God would help her speak to these pastors. Many would be walking miles over mountains; others would travel long distances by bus. She knew she had to have God's message for these pastors.

To her surprise she found Mark's picture mounted in several churches, and the mention of his name evoked awe and reverence.

Huldah was embarrassed by the kindness shown her. Shawls were presented representing the different tribes. And a government official loaned a car to escort her around in during her stay.

One night the driver brought the car to an abrupt stop. Soldiers had motioned the car to a halt. A bayonet was pushed through the open front window. "Where are you going?" a soldier asked. Then the back door was opened, and a soldier stared into Huldah's eyes. He smiled, closed the door, and waved them on. The driver was uncertain what had precipitated the roadblock, although there was a strictly enforced curfew because of tribal conflict.

Every afternoon, Huldah was taken to villages where she saw churches built with their own money and their own hands. These were self-sufficient, industrious people. Some congregations had named their church after Mark. It served to remind Huldah that her husband had not only touched lives in Calcutta; he had also touched the lives of hundreds in other areas of India.

Huldah preached ten sermons in three days. And the people weren't disappointed. They listened intently as she encouraged them to seek God for strong faith to believe that He would reach their villages with the love of Jesus Christ. Huldah was convinced they would have stayed all night had she continued speaking. The Lord had given her the right message at the right time. Tears filled her eyes as they clutched her hands warmly, standing in a long line to thank her after every service.

As the meetings came to an end, many thanked God for speaking to them, and for sending *another* messenger like Billy Graham and Mark Buntain.

CHAPTER TEN

40-Year Anniversary

October 6, 1994 was set aside to honor Huldah for 40 years of service and sacrifice. Dignitaries and friends had converged on Calcutta for the occasion. This would be a day to celebrate achievement, to thank God for sending Mark and Huldah Buntain to Calcutta.

About 1,500 employees and friends gathered in the church sanctuary. They greeted her with a standing ovation when she entered, amidst rows of flowers and special decorations. They all had their own stories to tell—how this woman had influenced their lives.

A videotape was shown featuring the remarks of young people, hospital patients, doctors, students, pastors, and orphans. Many told how the Buntains had rescued them from death and given them hope. "I don't know where I'd be without Pastor and Mrs. Buntain," many said.

Huldah was then presented with a stack of letters from friends around the world. A four-foot card filled with notes from schoolchildren was also presented. She then was handed the keys to a new automobile—a compact with air conditioning. This was a feature she had lived without for 40 years.

The Vision

The anniversary ceremony also featured musical selections from a children's choir and other groups. This was followed by speeches from pastors and foreign guests.

Then it was Huldah's turn to speak. She wept as she began recounting the history of the church and Mission. She couldn't help but wish Mark was present. "When we first came to Calcutta, we never dreamed God would choose to make this our home for 40 years," she said. "If Mark were here he would surely say, 'Thank you, precious Calcutta. We are indebted to you. We love you.' And please know we surely do love each one of you. We thank God for you. None of this would have been possible without you joining hands with us. To God be the glory."

While she was sharing there was no way she could have known what was happening to Dwain Jones, ministry representative for Mission of Mercy. Dwain had flown from the States to participate in the celebration.

This is how he later described what occurred:

I was sitting on the platform looking into the faces of the 1,500 precious Indian people who had been touched by the ministry of the late Dr. Mark Buntain. I thought to myself, *Oh, if Mark could only be here.* I was carried away by the presence of the Living Christ. Hot tears were streaming down my face. In a moment, I was lost in the sacredness of the moment; it was an experience like I had never known before. I was having a vision. I saw with clarity Mark Buntain rejoicing in heaven as if to be looking over the balcony, praising the God whose presence filled that room. He inhabited a body with no limitation, shouting inimitably, "Keep pressing on! Keep pressing on!" Mark looked at me and said, "Tell my sweetheart Huldah I love her and that I'm proud of her. Tell her that even though walking the streets of Calcutta daily is at times overwhelming, you soon will be with me dancing on streets of gold. Tell her that I'm sorry I didn't get to take her to the finest restaurants during our journey together in Calcutta, but that one day we will sit down at a banquet feast prepared just for us.

Tell her I'm sorry I was separated from her so much, but for 10,000 years, we'll reign in heaven with Jesus, never to be apart again. Tell the choir to keep singing and that, very soon, they will join a heavenly choir so great that the angels will have to stop and listen." As quickly as the vision came, it was gone. My heart was leaping within me. Because I was privileged to preach in that service, I shared with Huldah and the congregation the vision was no dream. To all who are faithful we will be going soon to a city where there will be no separation, no sickness, and no tears. One day we will join Mark and all the other great servants.

When Huldah learned of the vision, she felt unusual warmth and comfort. For an instant she wished she could see Mark's face, too. But as she scanned the large audience of friendly faces, she could see him in the smiles of so many. She was reminded that she and Mark had been part of a miracle—a miracle that had helped determine the eternal home of thousands. She found solace knowing that the miracles experienced on Park Street and in other areas were not only a testimony of God's faithfulness in years gone by; this church, Mission, and its people were living testaments of God's power today.

Making a Difference

Mark and Huldah came to Calcutta with a vision to help lost, needy people. They labored for years, touching one person at a time. The Buntains brought a powerful, liberating message that transcended the spoken Word to include meeting the basic human needs of hurting people. They ministered under the conviction that if the gospel is truly "good news," it has something to say to every aspect of life—not just spiritual concerns. It is the gospel of wholeness. They saw in the Scriptures God's identification with the weak and poor and His concern about the welfare of people. Matthew 25:35-40 (NIV), they claimed, was a command from the heart of God:

"For I was hungry and you gave me something to eat, I was thirsty and you gave me something to drink, I was a stranger and you invited me in, I needed clothes and you clothed me, I was sick and you looked after me, I was in prison and you came to visit me." Then the righteous will answer him, "Lord, when did we see you hungry and feed you, or thirsty and give you something to drink? When did we see you a stranger and invite you in, or needing clothes and clothe you? When did we see you sick or in prison and go to visit you?" The King will reply, "I tell you the truth, whatever you did for one of the least of these brothers of mine, you did for me."

The Buntains and Mission of Mercy, in obedience to God's Word, made a commitment to meet the physical and spiritual needs of people living in poverty-stricken areas of the world. They have labored for years to communicate love and freedom in Christ to people bound by starvation, lack of education, homelessness, poor health conditions, and empty religious traditions. That commitment and philosophy for ministry have reaped thousands of souls.

The Heart of God

Mark Buntain, speaking at the Assemblies of God General Council in 1967, reiterated his commitment to the lost and hurting:

I am proud to share the wonderful story of the Master's love with the people I have learned to love with all my heart, the people of the great land of India. I am humbled to be His missionary in the great and needy city of Calcutta. Let us stand and face this world with its darkness and its needs and stand with deep appreciation of the cry. I thank my God that it won't be long before the trumpet will sound.... We must give an account of the opportunity placed into our hands by the Holy Spirit to reach men and women with the only gospel that can give them hope, that can give them peace and eternally save their soul.... May we see men and women as God sees them today. May we see them as they are bound with the chains of spiritual darkness. May we see them in their physical and in their material plight.... World missions must come first in our heart, in our life, and in everything that we do.

God's Plan for Calcutta

When the Buntains came to Calcutta, they were confronted by children living in squalid poverty and despair. "Dear Lord," Huldah said then, "help me to make a difference here. The need is so great." That night she claimed the promise of Proverbs 16:3: "Commit to the Lord whatever you do, and your plans will succeed" (NIV). God has honored that prayer. He gave the Buntains His plan and they responded in obedience. What has resulted is nothing short of a miracle.

1954
Mark and Huldah Buntain arrived in Calcutta.

1954-55
Tent meetings were conducted every night on the property at Royd Street, which was later purchased for the church.

1956
Services were moved to the Revival Center—a hall above a restaurant and bar on Park Street.

1958
Because one billion of the world's 5.2 billion are illiterate, Mark and Huldah believed radio ministry was essential. Having once worked as an announcer at a Canadian radio station, Mark had the experience to launch a successful program. The Mission's radio ministry began broadcasting in English over the Far East Broadcasting Association.

1959
No longer was the congregation having to meet in a tent or rented hall. God provided property to build a new church on Royd Street. Christmas Day the new facility was dedicated.

1964

Realizing how important children were to Jesus, the Buntains started a grade-level school with 230 students. Quite often Mark could be found standing at the school door, shaking hands and greeting each student personally as he or she entered.

Enrollment rose to 500 by the end of the year. As the school became known, hundreds of parents would stand in line to apply for admission of their children.

1964

In an effort to reach Calcutta's leading businessmen with the gospel, a Breakfast Fellowship was started. In the years following, a Young Women's Fellowship was also launched.

1965

Seeing malnourished children falling asleep in the classroom, a feeding program was started for the students. The morning meal featured chapattis (a nourishing pancake) and milk.

1965

Hindi-speaking people came to the English-speaking church services just to sit in God's presence. They couldn't understand the preaching of Pastor Buntain, but they felt the moving of the Holy Spirit. Finally a Hindi section of the church was started in the home of one of the Buntains' most faithful parishioners.

1965

The radio program was so successful that Mark began airing it in Bengali, which brought immediate response from all over India. Hundreds of letters from thankful listeners arrived at his office.

1968

Wanting to declare the birth of Jesus Christ to a city, the Buntains started "Songs of the Season." The Christmas musical, featuring a choir and drama, attracted thousands each year.

Today the program is performed as an outdoor "singing Christmas tree." Life-size images of the manger scene and lights are positioned so thousands of people in Calcutta can hear about the story of Jesus' birth. Another featured program following "Songs of the Season" is the "Christmas Story in Sound and Light." The Christmas story is told in English, Hindi, and Bengali, and literature is distributed to each one who attends.

1968

The Telegu-speaking section of the church was started.

1968

Churches were planted in the villages of Thakurnagar, Guma, and Bongaon. This created a need for Christian schools that were started in each of these areas.

1968

An advocate of the written word, Mark laid plans to start a printing department that could produce and distribute gospel and educational literature. Today all the literature for the ministry, including International Correspondence Institute material, is printed by the Mission's press.

1969

A Hindi-speaking medium school was opened for children living in the slum areas of Calcutta. Through the years this school has reached thousands of families by feeding, clothing, and educating children. Many children are bathed and their tattered clothes replaced with clean uniforms when they arrive at school.

1970

Bible studies from International Correspondence Institute began being distributed in English and Bengali. Eventually it expanded to seven offices and spread to the states of Orissa, Nagaland, Manipur, Tripura, and Assam. Studies were distributed in many languages. Today, more than 500,000 are enrolled in the correspondence courses.

1970

The Bengali- and Nepali-speaking sections of the church were started.

1971

Mark and Huldah witnessed people dying due to inadequate medical care and were led to start a small medical facility. It started in one room with two beds and was staffed by a few volunteer nurses and doctors. Mark maintained that Jesus was the human extension of God's hand, the One who heals all diseases. And today, as medical and surgical skills are continually developed and perfected, God is still the Healer who uses trained and untrained persons to do His work. The facility continued to expand, actively participating in disease prevention programs. Hundreds waited in line each day for vaccinations. The need was so great that Mark and Huldah began planning the construction of a major hospital facility.

1975

Bengali medium schools were opened in Dum Dum and Kaorapukur (suburban areas of Calcutta).

1976

The Tamil-speaking section of the church was started.

1977

Construction of the six-story Hospital and Research Center was completed on Park Street. Mobile medical units were later dispatched to treat villagers.

1977

The Buntains searched for months to locate a building to start a home for boys. They wanted a facility where they could care for orphaned, abandoned, and abused children. A newspaper ad was placed indicating their desire to lease or purchase a building. A property owner replied to the ad the first day it ran; he invited the Buntains to inspect the available facility. When the owner learned the Buntains wanted the building to care for underprivileged children, he and his wife were anxious to make it available at an affordable price.

1977
Churches were opened in the West Bengal villages of Kestopur, Taherpur, and Ashokenager. This was followed by starting Bengali medium schools in each of these areas.

1979
The School of Nursing was inaugurated. Many nurses have been assisted with this training through the years and are working in the Mission hospital. The school is affiliated with the West Bengal Nursing Services and is a recognized program.

1981
The Oriya-speaking section of the church was started.

1981
A home for the aged and destitute was opened at Royd Street, where a good number of homeless, elderly people have received housing and care.

1981

A Bengali medium school was started in Maslandapur to coincide with the construction of a new church.

1982

The education ministry expanded to 12 schools with an enrollment of more than 3,000 children. It has now expanded to 21 schools and 10,000 students.

1982

The feeding program expanded to five locations when Mother Teresa took Mark to the local garbage dump and asked him to consider starting a feeding program there. That day Mark witnessed families rummaging through garbage for morsels of food. He promptly arranged for trucks to begin taking food out to this area and other locations every morning. Cooks were hired to prepare food all night so it would be ready for morning delivery.

1986

The Buntain Education Center and the 10-story A.G. Towers were built at the Park Street location. The education facility provides adequate classroom space in the five-story school building. The A.G. Towers provides administrative offices on the top two floors and School of Nursing classrooms and more administrative offices on the ground floors. Today the education facility also houses the Teachers' Training College and vocational school.

1986

West Bengal Bible College was actually established in 1962 to impart biblical truth to men and women who were called to spread the gospel. In 1986 the college began with a degree program that would later be accredited by the Asia Theological Association. Since then hundreds of students have walked through the commencement line to receive a bachelor of theology degree. The college also offers a diploma and certificate in theology. The institution is bilingual, offering courses in English and Bengali.

Speaking at graduation exercises, Huldah said in 1994: "You are called not to a job or career, but to a lifetime of ministry. To earn a passing mark in God's eyes, we must be willing to risk ourselves for His call and be willing to put our complete faith and trust in Him. Don't settle for less than God's best. Life in God's sight is risking yourself, not playing it safe, but playing it sacrificially."

Until 1993 classes were held in the A.G. Towers and in the Buntain Education Center. The new facilities in the lower floor of the church were dedicated in 1993. More than 90 percent of the graduates are in full-time ministry.

1986

The hospital was expanded to 150 beds with the formation of a new pediatric ward. Later it expanded to 167 beds. Quarters for the students in the School of

Nursing were also constructed on the fifth floor of the hospital.

1987
Recognizing the need to provide job training for young people, the Buntains established a vocational school. More than 2,000 graduates have entered the work force as secretaries, radio-television repairmen, dressmakers, fashion designers, cooks, and caterers.

1988
The Malayalam-speaking section of the church was started.

1988
A Teachers' Training Junior College was founded. The college has since dispatched many teachers to serve in the Mission's schools and in other institutions.

1989
Mark Buntain passed away June 4, 1989. Huldah Buntain was named chairman and senior pastor.

1989
The intensive care unit was opened at the hospital, thereby making it possible for doctors to treat more patients in critical condition.

1990
A three-story residence for students attending the School of Nursing was purchased. Bonnie Long, a

nurse herself, dedicated the building in memory of her father Mark Buntain.

1990

The first Hindi and Nagpuria radio programs were broadcast over Far East Broadcasting.

1991

A satellite cell ministry was started, permitting smaller groups to gather in their respective areas of Calcutta for Bible study and fellowship. The following year the cell groups expanded to six locations.

1992

Outreach churches and preaching points expanded to 48 locations. Ten more were added in 1994.

1992

A number of construction projects were initiated in outreach areas of West Bengal. The church's outreach ministries expanded to North Bengal. In Darjeeling a new church building was constructed and many village churches in the mountains were established.

Areas coming under the supervision and jurisdiction of Huldah Buntain extended to include West Bengal, North Bengal, South Bihar, Orissa, and the seven states of East India.

1992

Another school was built and dedicated in the village of Guma.

1992

The Orissa ministries expanded amongst the fishermen's villages. Churches were also opened in major cities. A number of schools and daycare centers were established.

1992

The first Oriya gospel radio program was broadcast over Far East Broadcasting.

1993

Mark Buntain Memorial Assembly of God Church was completed and dedicated.

1993

The cardiac care unit was installed at the hospital.

1994

After visiting some villages, Huldah noted that many churches were being pastored by untrained workers. She returned to Calcutta feeling the burden to start extension Bible schools. Soon they were opened in the following locations: Ranchi, Bihar; Darjeeling, North Bengal; Puri, Orissa; Kohima, Nagaland; and Jorhat, Assam.

1994

Through the feeding ministry, more than 20,000 women and children were receiving food six days a week.

1995

Mission of Mercy has 50 schools in West Bengal, South Bihar, Orissa, and in the seven states of East India. Six children's homes care for 250 boys and girls. Daycare centers tend to children in Orissa. Mark and Huldah always believed in the importance of reaching India's youth. That philosophy continues to permeate the church's efforts. More than 500 teenagers attend the annual youth convention. About 1,800 young people participate in 18 youth camps each year. Hundreds attend the annual youth conference and vacation Bible school.

Ambassadors in Mission teams go out during the holiday months—when schools and colleges are closed—to assist the village churches.

The Future

Huldah is often asked how she and Mark were able to accomplish so much for the kingdom of God. Routinely she responds, "We took it one day at a time. We worked hard, and we tried our best to listen to the voice of God. But truthfully we were just instruments. This was all in God's plan. He's the One who sent us; He's the One who performed the miracles; He's the One who sustained us. This is truly His work. And because of that, I have no worries for the future. This church and Mission are in His hands."

Tent revival meeting in 1957.
Mission of Mercy Archives

Dr. and Mrs. Mark Buntain
Mission of Mercy Archives

The congregation outside its second location—
The Calcutta Revival Center.

Mission of Mercy Archives

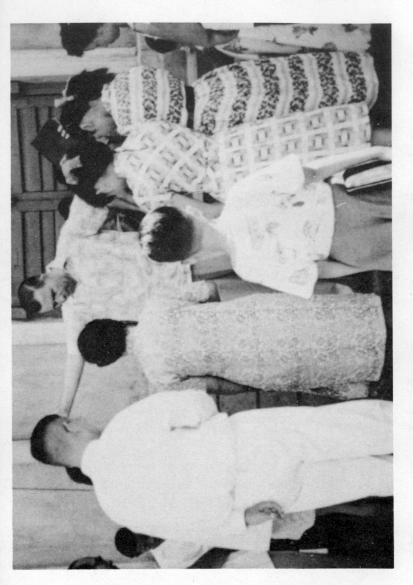

Mark Buntain praying for the sick in 1955.

Mission of Mercy Archives

**Huldah Buntain with Mother Teresa
at the grave of Dr. Mark Buntain.**

Mission of Mercy Archives

Huldah Buntain welcomes participants at the
Twelfth Annual School of Nursing Graduation.

Mission of Mercy Archives

Students at the Mission of Mercy school.

Mission of Mercy Archives

Huldah stands with students who attend
the Mission of Mercy school.

Mission of Mercy Archives

Dr. Mark Buntain

Mission of Mercy Archives

Calcutta, India

Mission of Mercy Archives

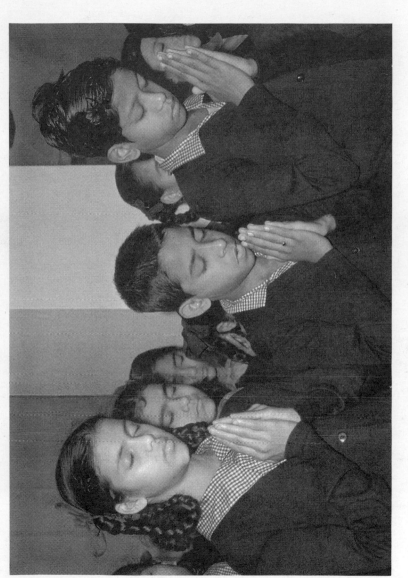

Young people praying in chapel.
Mission of Mercy Archives

Mark, Huldah, and Bonnie in 1965.

Mission of Mercy Archives

Huldah at one of the feeding sites.

Mission of Mercy Archives

Huldah with David Burdine and Don Beard.

Mission of Mercy Archives

Worship service at West Bengal Bible College.

Mission of Mercy Archives

Hindi Medium School celebrates 25-year anniversary.

Mission of Mercy Archives

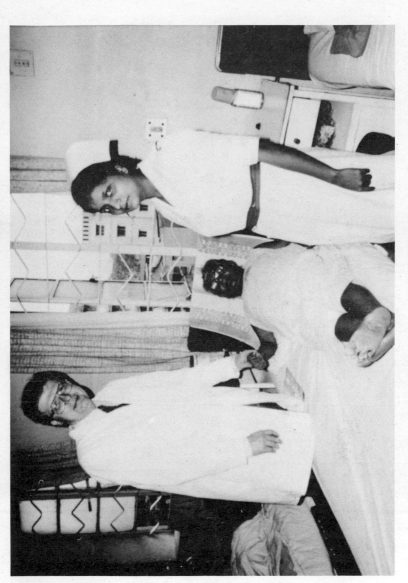

Dr. Jim Long visits a patient at the Mission hospital.
Mission of Mercy Archives

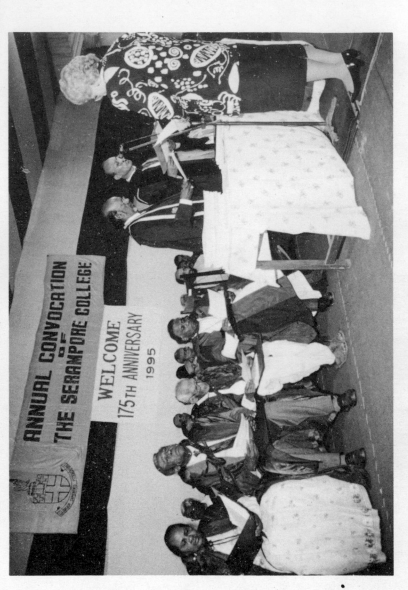

Huldah receives a doctor of divinity degree which was posthumously conferred on Mark by Serampore University.

Mission of Mercy Archives

Huldah speaking to her congregation.
Mission of Mercy Archives

Feeding the hungry.
Mission of Mercy Archives

A Message from Bob Houlihan, President, Mission of Mercy:

Mark and Huldah Buntain have been an inspiration to people around the world. Through them and their supporters, Jesus has fed, educated, and clothed thousands. He has revealed himself to countless people and rescued many more living in despair. This ministry has been possible because friends around the globe have joined hands with Jesus to reach out to the lost and hurting of India, and beyond.

Consider joining hands with Mission of Mercy today. As a result of the Buntains' outreach to Calcutta, Mission of Mercy currently is working in more than 25 nations on four continents. Many will be in heaven because of your compassion and action. Thank you in advance for your participation.

Order Form

You can help hurting people and be blessed at the same time by ordering one of these Mission of Mercy releases:

☐ *Treasures in Heaven,* by Huldah Buntain. Huldah reveals her personal struggles and private victories. ($10 donation suggested per copy)

☐ *Hold Up The Light.* Robert Solomon sings beautiful songs of worship. ☐ cassette tape ($10 donation suggested) or ☐ CD ($15 donation suggested)

Please send me _____ additional copies of *Woman of Courage.* ($10 donation suggested per copy)

Please send me the items indicated. I have enclosed a donation of $_____ to cover the items requested.

I don't wish to order any items, but I've enclosed my gift of $_____ to help hurting people.

Name _____

Address _____

City_____ State_____ Zip_____

Send all requests to:

Mission of Mercy
P. O. Box 62600
Colorado Springs, CO 80962

☐ YES!

I WANT TO BRING NEW LIFE IN CHRIST TO A NEEDY CHILD. I WOULD LIKE TO:

☐ Sponsor a child for $25 a month
    ☐ boy   ☐ girl   ☐ either

☐ Make a one-time gift toward Mission of Mercy's children's crisis fund.

☐ $50   ☐ $25   ☐ $15   ☐ $75
☐ $100   ☐ $500   ☐ $1,000
☐ other $_____

Name _____

Address _____

City _____ State _____ Zip _____

Telephone _____

Church Affiliation _____

Send to:
Mission of Mercy
P. O. Box 62600
Colorado Springs, CO 80962

About the Editors

Hal Donaldson is the editor of the *Pentecostal Evangel* and a graduate of Bethany College and San Jose State University. He is president of Convoy of Hope. He has authored 19 books.

Kenneth M. Dobson received his B.A. in Biblical Literature from Northwest College and his M.A. in Church Leadership from Southern California College. He formerly served with Mark and Huldah Buntain in Calcutta, India. He has authored or compiled six books. He is president of The Purpose Institute.